The Chicken Shop Incident

by Daniel Best

[redacted]

The Chicken Shop Incident

Written by Daniel Best

Cover artwork by Daniel Best

This is a work of creative nonfiction. The events are portrayed to the best of Daniel Best's memory. While all the stories in the book are true, some [redacted] been changed to protect [redacted].

This book is an [redacted] in its entirety, without the use of artificial [redacted] writing assistants.

[redacted] 2023
Second impression, with minor extensions April 2024

[redacted]

[redacted]

To Fred and Julie, for what I put you through.

To Corina and Ryan, who can understand this.

To Rio, Sia and Rocco, for when you're old enough.

To my friends, the victims.

Dark Times

I have done many terrible things in my life. When you have reached a certain age, for some at least, that is a given. The path that has heretofore led me where I am now has been fraught with terrible things. In paying heed to the legacy of the pill-popper, the dope smoker, or the dust snorter, I suppose that I would say the experience of normality is the most terrible thing of all. Some of us are scared of normality, and as a previous partaker in class A's I can say I know the feeling. It is therefore quite a lucky circumstance that I can say I rarely face it, as such. In fact, as you will see, the situation I had before me has a little essence of the divine to it, and a psychedelic one, and a bland one all at once. As you will see!

There are several places at which I could start, any of which would help in our investigation into what exactly happened in my life, which I am interested in, and which could be of some insight to you. I do not know where it will take us, and neither do I know what will come of it, but I think that because it has such a pressing urgency in my own mind, and that it causes me the most unsettling distress, and because it could well be the best way to start, I will tell you of the darkest period of my life. Yet even here I could write of that penultimate crime which I committed straight away, or go even further back, which I will, to that darkest of dark realms – my bedroom in Colindale, 2006.

Now, here we are on the double bed that was in the corner of the room, and it is December, just after my twenty eighth birthday, and I am gazing at the walls, the bookshelf, the poster of anime classic Howl's Moving Castle, and the computer that sits upon the desk before the small window. My room is a total mess: there are coke bottles long since emptied lying alongside take away wrappers courtesy of the local grill, all strewn across the floor. There are papers and books, and correspondence from utility companies, and my head is tense.

My head is tense, and I am searching for a heaven that was once here. The walls have photos of family, a certificate of achievement from a college, and are flecked with bits of spat out tobacco and snot. I am writing by means of my computer an email of sorts: a letter to a website dedicated to philosophy. This is the subject that I have chosen to study at university.

My head is tense and with every word I write I see a new angel in heaven, and a king, and many virgins. But they are not there. They are unclear.

The topic of discussion is the existence of God, a topic so popular on this website that a 'thread' could last a thousand replies. Yet I have my own topic to talk of. The subject of God's existence is a cover for the image I have in my head, of gamers' favourite, Super Mario. Something has convinced me that I can put this image in the mind of the reader, merely by words. Yet there is frustration... I am far away from my goal, which is to attain heaven – the heaven that *was*. My letter is failing, and I am far away from my goal. My head is tense because of my incapacity to explain what I need to explain, and the pressure of going to university, and what I know. There were some at that institution whom I felt I could indeed relate to, it being some special knowledge that I knew, and others knowing it too. Doctor Lawson, a university lecturer who knew everything there is to know about philosophy, could reassure me, as could Martin P., a student so at ease in these surroundings, who was not a mature student as I was, and who wrote essays in the way that I wanted to – in the way I thought I did.

Yet two people among a thousand were hardly enough to completely emancipate me from my own troubles. Hence the pressure of going to that place was rarely alleviated. And all the while I would look about myself and think of these kids - too clever, too quick, too cool, too young! - I would think how lovely it is to be here. And, in lectures and seminars, I could think highly of myself, that I had made it there. But that pressure! I'm talking about that unconscious knowledge that requires we behave according to institution, and says, 'You have not yet thought! You have not yet thought! It was clear that I hadn't, yet still I was there among people much younger, cleverer, quicker and more suited to this environment. I almost cannot source the stress.

Also, reassuringly, there were other mature students. Mick, the cocky beer lad, cocksure to hide insecurity, could simply not relent, or acquiesce in the unbelievable notion, that *I* could be clever, and who did not even seem that clever himself, and who disliked me, I suppose. Jane, who was at this college despite her own misgivings, yet who possessed an academicism about her, and who I would kiss in a state of psychosis. Michael, the saving grace of my entire university career, who mentioned me to the counsellor because I had attempted suicide. These three would be the first to whom I would show my cuts, all stitched and bandaged, like a surplus head. I was not cut out for college life, said something inside of me when I went there, but I would need that degree, that qualification, that credential.

Every time I would walk down that "Street", that stretch of pavement inside the college, there would be new reason for stress. So naive was I that I took it on, I played along with the game, I absorbed it. I did that, and found in the end that uni-life was not what I had expected. Such inner turmoil is possessed of the uni-youth that there was little coherence in that tacit conversation we were all having, that I laughed.

One day, sitting and trying to access my intraweb page via a password that would keep failing, I laughed. I laughed so hard that it was a wonder how nobody raised an eyelid. And hard I laughed knowing just how out of my depth I was; yes, I knew even then, yet persisted. That's one of my better attributes – I'm persistent. I laughed at the work I had to do; I laughed at my lack of uni-sensibility; I laughed at them and I laughed at myself. It was a laugh of distress, of exasperation, of sadness. It was a laugh of stupidity. The computer would not play my game; and I laughed. Did anyone know I was laughing? I think they did not.

"Why did you do that?" asked my social worker after my suicide attempt.

It was a good question, and one I could only answer, "To relieve people of the burden of me!"

In any case, my mind being of the state in which I could not stop writing until I gained that elusive insight into the afterlife I pined for, and not being allowed to sleep until then (my own rule), I continued pressurising myself in that bedroom in Colindale in 2006 in the darkness. On occasion, the guesses I made about that insight were in the correct quadrant, yet there was an urgency and an impatience that intermingled with my own pious concerns. Even at that time I was mentally convinced that it might be good to see my peers along the same course of life that life had taken me. It was simply necessary. There were no two ways about it. And after everything that had gone on, after all the pain and distress, I still loved God. That's the thing. Having such experiences that would never leave my mind, I still loved Him! I would make excuses for the events that had happened. I would say, "God is about reality; He keeps it real." This outlook would serve to keep me in consistent world view for such time that in the end I had to forget about reality. But that's all ahead. For now, the thing was stress.

The thing about the stress I felt at that time was its strange, intellect placating character. It sort of usurped my consciousness so that I even felt I *could* think, which was my goal. But I still could not think! That day, sat before the PC in my bedroom in Colindale in 2006, I could see the angels, the princes, the virgins, all teasing me that their glory was all but beyond my reach. All I needed was that key word, that phrase, that insight – and in a sense even I didn't know what I needed – and it wasn't coming. There was every thought at my disposal! I knew enough that I could communicate, but only on a human level; I was out for the divine, and I was in good company, the sign of which was that incessant conviction that you know better than your peers. Sleep was not the order of the day. I had to write and write, and not merely for the college. It was a Saturday night. I had to write and write. I needed some insight.

But how is a genius to rest? 'Perhaps,' I thought, 'I should l lay down and close my eyes for a minute, just so I could carry on in a moment.'

I woke up several hours later from a dream about Jesus, about Muslims, about Jews and about persecution, with what can only be described as a "brain-stench", that was so ghastly and so deathly, a smell that told me I might have 'bought it' last night, yet so beautiful it could only have come from the heavenly father. It was also strong, and since I had woken up in the very same position in which I had gone to sleep, I knew I must be chosen. Whatever dream I'd had that night I knew I had to go out into the public today and greet everyone. So that became my plan. I would go to Golders Green and visit some synagogue and open my arms to some rabbi who would see my love, my capacity for forgiveness, my peace. I left the flat and I took the bus to town, which I walked with higher knowledge and that wisdom which came with a rested mind.

Now, I may or may not have been thinking, but I felt, in so many words that I could see people's thoughts. Here, there is always the sense that I've finally 'got back' to that place I once was, and the first regret came, on that sunny, cold Sunday, when I made my first encounter. It was at a bus stop where there was a young lady and a builder. I wanted to open up to the lady first of all, yet she was timid and scared and I had not the language she needed. Happier was she when I turned to the builder (a Pole) and began to talk to him about pigeons, the ones there. Yes, the woman was happy then, but the circumstance was unfitting, so then I was sad, but the bus came, and I made my way.

I remember the sun on that Sunday, shining into the bus's windows atop the higher deck, and I remember the Polishness, and the Africanness, and that effeminate naivety at helpless innocence. Not a Jew to be seen. I remember the morning nuances of the London underground, with travellers so impressed, or so indifferent, at my character, that I found myself near St. Paul's Cathedral, with my satchel, inside which were some sketch pads, and there were some early morning skateboarders, BMX bikers, roller skaters, and I walked.

This is that 'proverbial wander' that is infamous for being a symptom of illness, until the criminal is finally caught, to be taken where doctors are. It starts in innocence with a purchase of tobacco, leads through, usually, High Barnet, and winds up with you in trouble at some police station. And the ten o'clock sunlight shone on the building's sides, and the streets were Sunday clean. The buildings were so high, the streets so quiet; I had never been here before. And there were Sunday workers: some blue collar, some white. I perched at a bench and rolled a fag and saw the cathedral in Westminster, all covered in scaffold and sheets, and I took out a pad and pen and drew a sketch of that erection which, to look at, would never have caused the least amazement to anybody. Two labourers worked nearby. A bus drew past. In fact, I sat very close to a bus stop and soon, having thought for some time, had the realisation that women did not, for their lives, know about how beautiful they are, or at least did not know how lovely men can find them.

Now, I do not know whether there is such a thing as psychic ability, but that day I got to the notion that there is at least an element of it in the natural communication of society. I realised how to say it – how to tell women of their beauty – merely by a look. What you do, is you think the opposite of the notion you wish to impart, and qualify it with a signature arrival notice that can only be explained in dreams – a sign, if you will, from higher thought. And upon this notion a bus drew by, with a studious looking piece of pussy a top the higher deck, looking at me and smiling with a nod when I communicated, "Ugly here!!" She had instantly understood; I had made her happy. The force of my realisation had, indeed, made several other women similarly happy, and this was a kiss.

Yet there was a pressure coming from those pair of labourers, one of whom had sat down next to me on the bench for a chat. He was drinking coffee (wasn't he?) and eating a tuna sandwich, and he made mention of ghosts – ghosts and spirits – perhaps inspired by the holiness of St Paul's Cathedral. But he was not genuinely clever. Sitting next to me, however, perhaps made him feel clever; but sitting next to him made me feel as if I was dead. The conversation we had that day could well have been about politics, about the queen, about construction, but his large nose and grey head, his misplaced condescension, his disdainful manner, was such that I was left feeling, although glad of the encounter, somewhat despondent, indeed, depressed. I was already depressed! His friend loitered around while this hulk of a fart arsey beast began to aggravate me quite a bit and

I wanted him to fuck off! Despite our talk of royalty and ghosts he seemed to think me dumb, that I had no idea what I was doing, when the opposite was the case. In any case, he went back to work on this relatively quiet street, doing some shuttering on trestles and, every so often, I could feel his glare on my head, obviously thinking himself better than I. I waited till he and his farty workmate went round a corner out of sight before I fucked off down the road. It was a farty time indeed.

Despite that, I managed to communicate my inner appreciation of female beauty to many ladies that day, even if I had to jam my tongue up right into the roof of my mouth to do so. Here was the insight I had been looking for, and thus was the beginning of my tirade against ignorant, sexually repressed men, to the exaltation of females wherever they may be.

As sunny, cold Sundays go, it was not the most amazing day, to be fair. Yet it stands out in my mind as one of those socially glorious days of interaction that serves to absolutely confirm your social importance in the world – a bit like if you were famous. However, it was also a day of stress, much of which came as the culmination of a summertime of desperate loneliness and mad craziness. In the summer of 2006 my Welsh uncle asked me to visit him and my Welsh family over in Wales. Being a onetime plasterer of walls I was expected to go there and work two days to render his extension, which I didn't mind because I would be paid. So he got me down there.

It was okay for the first few days, but if I've learned one thing from the experience it's that you should never go to Wales for more than three days. It's so sparse, and the communities seem to produce a lot of undesirables. There seem to be very tight restrictions on the matter of dealing with the latter, and they don't like outsiders. I just want to say that on one of the evenings I may or may not have found phlegm in my curry sauce. It may or may not be entirely obvious to say I was most stressed and was even traumatised by the experience, most of which was so tacit that I have failed to describe it in full. In any case, I was so relieved to be back in busy, thriving London town that I cried on the tube home. (I had even started crying from relief, long before that, on the coach from Cardiff). I cried when I made eye contact with someone, or even could have made eye contact with someone, or someone walked past. Nevertheless, even though I was back home, that feeling of having been smacked on the head with a falling brick full of stress had remained. It was a terrible feeling.

A little while after that was the time I went for a lovely camping trip up in New Forest. What was supposed to happen was that one of my best friends was meant to phone me one morning, and we were to go to Brighton to camp and drink. When the time came, inevitably, she fucked me off: she didn't call, and went without me. Years later it would transpire that this friend had been instructed by my ex-girlfriend (who was also going on the trip) to ignore my calls because she herself was going to have sex with some other person, and consequently didn't want me in the way.

So I ran away to New Forest to console myself. I hadn't even taken a torch, and when it got dark I had to sit under the light of the washing block to read. I remember the book I had been reading was "Being and Nothingness" by Jean Paul Sartre. I didn't manage to take the whole thing in that time, but I absorbed at least a few of the wise ideas therein. One which particularly stood out was something called "facticity", Sartre's own terminology, meaning, as far as I could gather, that relation between cause and effect. I understand this to be like the feeling of wetness: we don't feel wetness; we feel a warm or cold slipperiness – but not "wetness". I imagine wetness to be a sort of an inner sensation, like facticity, and it turns out I'm not talking bollocks, but that there is actually a relation between cause and effect which is by and large an inner perception. Anyway...

So, in short, I'd had a horrible summer, during which I never got round to studying particle physics as I expected I would, it being the case that I had just finished an access course in humanities. As sunny, cold Sundays go, it was not the most amazing day! It stands out in my mind because it was close to being one of those days that, if your life has gone downhill ever since, you want to get back to. We may begin a day with totally different expectations than which they end. I had started this one with the hope of getting more positive attention from the public than I could dream of. All I can say is that, on the final bus home, I stood reading Aristotle's Nicomachean Ethics, next to a young mother whose attention I had tried to get by reading each page very quickly; I had to: I was a genius after all.

She did not even notice. Well, she may have glanced at me. She must have, otherwise why would I remember that? In any case, I got home and ate a burger from the local grill house. The next day I had a philosophy lecture.

Old Sledgehammer Feet

Strange thoughts about death, the afterlife, and heaven abound in the mind of a young madman. There are reasons why men go mad.

I said that university was not ideal for me, but I think it even could have been, in the right circumstances. But, whatever happened during those three months of cerebral violence, one day I found myself on grey, bleak morning, awoken from this dream of blindness which put me in a bad mood. Indeed, I was annoyed.

That bus stop over from my flat, that took me to Burnt Oak, well, there was a man at it. A nobody. I wasn't right headed. I was beginning to know it. Schizophrenics can act on their most negative thoughts, and I was midway from being a hard nut slash student slash sicko and in case you missed it the first time - there was a man. A nobody.

From his perspective it would probably have been an

ordinary morning. He would sit his forty five year old behind at the seat, then look at some traffic, look up the road, down it, see the 142 and get on the 142 and go to work. A normal day. Then there are psychotics.

In my mind (made up to wreak revenge upon the thoughtless bullies of women, who needed to be woken up in some way or another), he knew exactly what he was doing: He was obviously a hateful fucker, that would use women, and was getting away with it. This fact was frustrating to me, and actually, in his own mind he probably knew little. I watched him, fuming with anger at his ignorance, made clear by his grey tracksuit, and large aquiline nose, and bulging eyes. I knew I hated him. In another world I would feel sorry for him – only, not this one. He was weak and I was strong. I could see his life of getting on buses and now and then reading a news paper. (In fact, if he was reading a news paper I might just have let him alone.) The bus arrived. He got on and I got on after him and sat at the back, opposite him. He was ignoring me, I was sure, in a purposeful way. I'm making excuses for myself now, but he was making me very angry. His dull blue eyes glaring out the window and the way his mouth was slightly open. I dealt with the situation right up until we arrived at Burnt Oak at which point my anger overflowed and I punched him in the nose.

"Oh!" he exclaimed, covering his face with his hands.

I jumped off the bus and ran up the road, feeling invincible. My hand was bleeding from the connecting blow, and I was escaping. But I had to get back into Burnt Oak one way or another – the way to do it was to catch the Uno bus which would go through town to the university. The bus arrived and I went upstairs and hid at the back, for I knew the bus would pass a commotion caused by me. It did, and at that bus stop I saw the unfortunate man sitting with his nose in a tissue, and a police car and policeman no doubt on the radio in search of me. I had escaped.

The Uno bus drove along its normally strenuous and stressful route all the way to Hatfield Business Park where I would alight and go into the wide forecourt of the University of Hertfordshire. Excited by the events of the morning I began to have ideas. They were all crazy ones all about what trouble I might find myself in as I watched the students passing through the area. I would have a cigarette.

I must have seemed of interest to at least two female students there for, as I buzzed about, smoking, they beckoned me to them, in a friendly way.

I just want to say about women in general that they are the most mysterious and lovely creatures on the planet, and that is the way I thought that day. Mysterious because what it is like to be around them can leave a man at odds with himself, or leave him in a perfect situation. My resolution for that day was that I need not speak at all. For what does a man need to say? Nothing. Actions say everything. And mine were that I flitted on my feet with a mind to engender a feeling of having fun with these forlorn looking young people.

So they beckoned me over. I had made the decision to not talk yet, but perhaps we spoke (in any case, it felt as if we did). We did, and it might have been about courses, classes, tutors. However, I think I stayed quiet. I did – I was shtum. Nevertheless I looked at these beautiful ladies, both with brunette hair, as they discussed their day, and they talked of this and that. However, at one stage my decision was to kiss one of them.

I kissed her cheek.

"Thank you!" said she, with a smile that forewent embarrassment.

I kissed the next girl's cheek.

"Thank you!" said she, with a similar sentiment as the first. All were happy! 'So,' I wondered. 'It's acceptable to kiss girls that you don't know!'

A third girl arrived in the group, but I didn't kiss her. They chatted for a moment about classes and work and soon said goodbye, or something, somehow. And it was okay.

Now, I sometimes relate this story to others, and when I do I always say this: It's all very well kissing strange girls when you like, but it's a different matter when you try to kiss strange boys!

I mean, it was just an experiment to see what would happen, but indeed, after the occurrence with those ladies, I decided to try it on a lad. He was at the entrance to the university, talking to a friend and smoking a fag. He was an Indian chap, about twenty. I approached him, as like unto a mosquito, and made little attempts to get in close to him. As I became closer I began to blow little kisses. I was very close when he noticed me.

"What are you doing?" he enquired angrily. I replied by blowing more kisses, closer and closer all the time.

When I got really close he grabbed me and began pushing me backwards, an action to which I might have reacted with violence, but didn't. I allowed him to push me, and still blew kisses, as he said, "Fuck off!" Then a security guard got involved and took me aside and talked to me, but I still wasn't speaking. I think, however, he must have got some words out of me, because in the end, he escorted me to class. The Indian lad was still screwing, and a girlfriend of his was grinning cheekily at me as I passed them then. I got so close to class.

It was a short but playful walk, as I was escorted to the seminar that day; playful from an inward stance – I was sick (yet didn't quite exactly know), and with that comes a playful intent. I was not to talk. Women did not need me to talk, so it became my rule. I followed the security guard along the academic halls, past the classrooms, until we got to the one I was in. There, a gaggle of young ladies waited outside, all class mates, none familiar but one, Jane, a mature student. There was a deep blue hue in the hallway, an orange outline, and an ominous feeling. As yet I could not see whether our female counterparts knew their beauty. If one thing was for sure it was that today was not a day for misogyny. There were young men there, and Mick.

I caused no stir as I approached the gaggle. Despite their loveliness, their beauty, their intelligence, I still saw no sign of awareness on the ladies' part of this. I was not yet the gift of God to females! Still there was time.

Watching the security guard's hi-viz jacket, I got the sense of trouble. It was like being in the company of police. But we got to classroom, and the guard turned to me and said, "Okay then, that's it. That's all." Then looking at me in the eye he said, "Look after yourself," at which I knowingly nodded, and he left.

Security guards are like the police in many ways. But police are much worse.

I've relapsed before. My first relapse was in 2004, almost a year after I was first sectioned. The way it happened was like this: I had been taking my 200mg every morning and night for some months. Then one day I missed my dose. The feeling of that was one of tension and stress, but I knew that a dose would help. I had missed doses before; tension would be relieved upon administration. I thought that if I could get past this initial tension, miss a few more doses, then perhaps my thoughts would come back. In the end I missed about a week's medication, and first began to notice it when my life, my world, the universe at large, began to take on a phantasmagorical effect.

Reading the bible in my tiny bathroom and stumbling, therein, upon a name Gershon I had been wondering at, which was the name of an Hassidic Jew from the hospital, I got the sense that I was inside a fantasy chess game: 3D, no less, but all people were players, all pieces on different squares, in their rooms or where they happened to be. I heard thumping noises that came from the flat above mine, and also heard the banging of a roofer on some nearby house – they seemed to speak to me in a way that said, "Old Danny Boy here, he's the quickest thinker around. There's no denying it! At least, *I* can't beat him!" It was true; my mind was flying.

The usual story: I took a walk about the area, with the intention to explore this new found resonance, this return to genius, that I had discovered. I walked and walked and was in Mill Hill. I was by the station when I happened upon my sister's brown Ford Escort parked on the street, and I thought, 'It can't be coincidence, someone must have stolen it!' There was a policeman nearby, and I talked to him of my suspicions, yet he found no information concerning those. Then he said, "You look confused, sir."

When he took me to the police station, after some discussion, and we got outside the entrance, I said I didn't want to go in. This instance culminated in a physical struggle, and then some other policemen got involved, and they dragged me inside, and I somehow remember that I was injected with something – although I can't be too sure if that's right. In any case I found myself in a cell, for no apparent reason. And furthermore, the police, having carried me in there and held me down to take off my shoes, had gone out, locked the cell door, and left me in there with a broken metal watch strap. And for one reason or another I went at myself with that, and then a doctor came along, saw my wrist was injured and bleeding, and then I was at Barnet Hospital, stuck in a room, guarded by police.

I was in that room for several shifts of police time. By the third I was so exasperated that I punched one of the officers. (It was such a bad punch – I was so tired I literally watched my hand, thinking 'this is going nowhere') For your information they got me down, handcuffed me, and a nurse injected me with antipsychotics. It took several seconds to have an effect but the feeling was like that of first administration of medication – it hurt, but it was nothing new. My mind had clicked off. They sat me up and told me to look at the wall, but I looked at their feet, and I will always remember 'The Policemen's Feet'.

One detail of this last experience, that drew me to have sympathy towards police, was 'The Policemen's Feet'. I stared at 'The Policemen's Feet', still unable to get up, being cuffed and uncomfortable. A young officer decided to kneel at my side. He seemed to want to explain something to me. His hands were in the mode of exclamation, he looked at me in the eye, he said, "We're trying to get you out of here, mate. That's what this whole thing's about, you see. But what keeps happening is that you... we're trying to get you out of here. Now, I'm appealing to your good nature; I know you're not a bad person, but you insist on keeping our attention on you, mate. So what I'm gonna do is, mate, is I'm gonna leave you on your own now and see how you get on then. After that I'm gonna have to take you to the hospital. Is that alright? You understand?"

I nodded. And so they left me alone for a bit, and after a while I found myself being carted off in a wheel chair to a police wagon. There was a hive of police gathered there by the wagon door, and I was about to get in, when I felt an urgency. It was a need for some sort of closure, and it seemed pressing to the policemen too, and I glanced back. Among the policemen's faces, all looking childishly anxious about something, I saw my friend, the kneeling one. He seemed sheepish as our eyes made contact, and the urgency found closure with a final thought: - 'Silly bastard.'

So it was not so much 'the policemen's feet' as I watched the back of our security guard's hi-viz jacket, but there was a similar type of nuance. As he walked away, I felt I had escaped something, but the cheeky intent had not gone. In fact, as I had felt many times before, trouble was afoot. I mean, it could so easily not have been, but it was, and my decision not to talk probably didn't help. The tutor arrived, a young red-faced, shorn headed guy with a tweed jacket and an armful of papers, and unlocked the door with a glance around, and we followed him in.

I was not, but the tutor was talking, and as we took our seats he began passing out marked assignments at which time soon we discovered mine wasn't there.

Wasn't there? My mind ventured at the possibilities. Had it just been misplaced? Or was there possibly some deeper reason for its absence? Whichever the truth, I was all the more angry. I silently stewed in my seat about the situation.

Of course, before this, I had been asked to speak, for the tutor did not know my name, which was needed for registration. He got annoyed – "What is your name??" I moved over to his desk and pointed it out on the sheet before him. I sat back down.

Very aware was I at this time, of the psychology of the male academic, which seemed to be that if he could not face himself, then he would, inevitably, take it out on the female. Freud would back me up on that, I'm sure. It appeared to be happening here in this class of academics where we were, but the most number of the males were young. So I watched Mick, at once assessing my theory for empirical clarification, and also to feel the anger of its truth when I saw the mature student angrily glance to one of the female cohort whenever the knowledge of his frustration against them would occur to him, at the time when common sense tells you you would do, and this deeply affected me. I had seen the ladies in our class and I had looked. I had, without talking, either imagined that I had, or actually had read the mind of one particular girl, and thought her to be a genius!

"Is that what I am?" I'd read her to say matter of factly. It was right – I knew it.

Anger alleviated by that happy experience, I went back to my post of watching Mick, who would still exact his insecurities upon the peaceful females, by nervous and frequent glares.

Anger back, I decided I would punch him. So I stood up, to the momentary confusion of the class, and approached the person. He was instantly aware of the attack I was about to make upon him, and rather than stand up and defend himself, he rather pathetically fell backwards off his chair in terror.

"What are you doing??" shouted the tutor. "Get out!"

In any case, I had realised it was time for me to leave. I edged around the desks to go, but before I did, I made as though I was going to hit the tutor, then smirked as he flinched, and I left thinking, "Pussies!"

And still I was not talking as June came out to hand me my bag, which I'd left. I took to kiss her cheek, to which she'd said "Thank you," and she walked me to the bottom of the stairway. The university was indifferent, with students acting as homosexual as ever. It was a very gay university. Almost everyone there was bent. As much as I regret my actions, and knew that was the last day I'd ever go back there, I've always wondered what would have happened had my assignment been available. And though it was short, I always reflect on my time at Hertfordshire University.

Now funnily enough, after all that, I still wasn't done. As I recall, standing once again in that forecourt,

I began to feel overcome with sexual urges, and looking, observing the girls with their academic satchels and things to do with study, I felt so powerful, so above and beyond this society that I began to touch the people around me. I would reach for the shoulder of one woman, and she'd stop, and I'd smile, and she'd smile back and continue to walk. A woman with Swedish features walked by, her chest within grasp, and I contemplated my limits, and though I felt desperate, and though I got the sense it would have been okay, I did not breach that liberty. But the urge became frustration, and I thought I could take my clothes off right there in the light of day, and it would be alright. I interrupted one woman, and though older, she was still attractive, and I desired her, and it was as if she became conscious under my touch, and she said, "Oh, I was in my own world!" and she laughed. But I had nothing; I could not even sexually assault her.

Now to look at the last experience you might see the makings of a sex offender. I am not. I did not breach that liberty.

Now with an image in my mind showing some divine orgy in the street, and now also beginning to have messianic feelings, right in the centre, I moved on.

The bus stop was a hundred metres away. And now, here, we become confused (we do), and begin to wish to hurt other men. And we take cues from the minds of women.

The women are saying, "Hit 'im," "Lamp 'im," "Get

'im," and the looks of the men are, "Don't hit me!" There, leather jacket – here, a smiling, knowing woman. "Hit 'im".

'But... there would be no point?! Why are you saying this to me?'

"Hit 'im!" she goes. And there: an Indian student, heavy set and a little helpless – perhaps an IT student. I look at him as if to say, "I am gonna lamp you so hard..." The way he looks back at me is as if to say, "I know, and I deserve it." It was that look that told me that if I have to hit him, then that would be okay. The desire was almost too strong, and as he walked past, and I didn't hit him, then I felt terrible, like he'd won. And you know, my pride was so visibly damaged, that he probably felt like he'd won too.

So that's why, when I finally lighted the bus to sit at the back of the lower deck, I realised I had to have a fight.

I'm a fighter in psychosis. I have felt psychotic many times and fought many. I have punched, kicked, won and lost. (Mainly lost). And just as I'm not a sex offender, I'm not a racist. You do find all types of men, to meet, to fight, and yes, we are all different. The last time I fought a black dude I lost badly. Yes, he was some strong fucker.

The night before was a night of violence, and I had escaped a thorough beating from a mob of angry lads, which was not a good thing. Mum told me to go and look for a job, that day. My plan, after last night's experience, was to keep myself to myself. I was sure I was going through a phase, and felt I had to stay out of trouble. I shuddered as the realisation set in.

So, walking into Mill Hill Broadway, I could do one of two things. I could actually go to the job centre or I could go to the building site of my dad's latest job – almost finished, and little there to do, but at least that would keep mum happy and me busy for the day. I decided to actually go to the job centre.

This decision had meant that it was necessary to walk past the bus stop that would otherwise have gone to dad's job. In doing so, then I was sure I was going to the job centre.

With this certainty, perhaps, came a little arrogance? Perhaps there *was*, as I continued my walk to the station, where the bus could have taken me to Burnt Oak, where there was a job centre.

And a sign, here, that said, "Oi!" as I came to the end of a road. The entire town melded into one swirling density of words and bright colours, and the September sun beamed on her afternoon so happy it confused me, me being in some state of unsatisfied frustration, and I had to focus.

Then, as I focussed, a man came into view, just a little way off down the road – and he stalked back and forth on the pavement, and he was on the phone, and there he was, talking; he was among the public – and I knew I had to avoid him. Yet the more I tried to do that the harder it became. When I veered over to one side of the pavement to avoid him, and he seemed to want that side, I veered to the other and he veered with me, still boasting about business to somebody on his phone. So, at the penultimate moment, we clashed – in retrospect, more my fault than his – and I'd given a pretty heavy shove, and he yelled, "Hey! Hey! What's this!" And I walked on further, until a second later when I decided to turn around. I did that and went to him face to face.

Now, at this point, and in light of the previous evening, it would have been natural that I headbutt him. That would have finished it off, and I could have walked on. However, he was – well – his face looked too soft; too malleable. I took pity on this feature, and instead of headbutting, I chose to punch him. It was a particularly weak right and it had no effect other than to anger the man. He said, "Alright," with a sense of resolve, and pushed me backwards.

Now, I hadn't heard voices up till this point, but right then something in my head said, 'You'd better run!' However, my foot was sprained from jumping off of a seven foot tall fence in Finchley last week. I couldn't run, but in any case he would have caught me. In any case, he did catch me, and I next received what I now know as "The Beating of My Life"!

I remember the dash to escape, and the fellow's anger as he grabbed me, pushed me to the ground, and kicked me in the jaw. I remember the searing pain of that kick, and even the thought of the comparison I made of it with being struck by a sledge hammer. I remember the fear and loss at being a perpetual weakling to this man, who had smacked me several times across the head. I fell into the road and, thinking of the defensive moves made by cage-fighters, stuck my legs in the air, toward him, and held him off. My jaw was really in pain and I was in shock. "Get opp!!" the fellow yelled. I shook my head no. "Get opp!!"

"No!"

And then he strutted away.

It was over, and I got up and dusted myself off. In shock, I was approached by another man of average height and a kind, deeply concerned face; you know the type. "Do you want me to call the police?" he asked. Doubtlessly, he had not witnessed the entire scene. 'Why would I want you to call the police?' I asked myself. 'It was my fault.'

"Okay!" I said, dishevelled. "And can you call an ambulance? My jaw is broken."

I had walked on past the scene of the 'crime' and was looking back at my assailant who was, I must say, in his element. Yes, he was most pleased with himself for his achievement of beating me senseless. Furthermore, there were other men observing proceedings, who saw that I myself was a part of the situation, and who seemed to be looking me up and down as if to say, "*I* could have him!"

'Oh really?' I thought. 'You could, could you?' and I thought about starting a fight with them, yet didn't actually do it, so as not to disappoint my assistant, the kind, bald man.

With the police now arrived, and my shattered jaw in pain, and a crowd of bystanders there watching everything going on, I was taken aside by an officer, and the other fellow was being questioned by another officer, and we were twenty feet apart, and 'my' officer stood between us, and the paramedics were arrived, and were addressing me in the street.

Now, little did I realise, I was psychotic, and psychotic in only the most obtuse of ways. For when I was spoken to, I have to tell you, I was not always able to understand what was being said. So when the paramedic was explaining to me, "If you want to go to hospital, you can," I understood him as saying, "If you want to have another go at him, you can!"

Still though, I wasn't sure if this interpretation was true; whether there were legalities allowing me this opportunity – and I still was not sure if 'to have another go at him' was my required course of action. So I waited for another sign; some indication of what they wanted me to do.

My officer was talking to me with his hands in motion, like some politician, and I couldn't focus on what he was saying. He was still stood between me and that fellow with the sledgehammer feet, and then, with quite a purposeful manner, like a theatrical curtain opening to reveal a show to eager eyes, the officer moved to one side; to the left of me. It was then I knew I was supposed to have my second 'police aided' 'go' at my new enemy.

Yet still unsure, and full of trepidation at the opportunity, I edged away from the police officer (in such a way as though I was asking, "Is this what you want me to do?"), and gradually towards old sledgehammer feet.

There was a shout, some calling, "Hey!" "Oi!" "Hey!" and I took a final look at the scene, and feeling tricked and really rather stupid, I was wrestled to the ground by several police, and my head lay jammed between the road and the pavement. "You see?!" cried my friend, to all the onlookers, with self righteousness. "You see?!" Old Sledgehammer feet was really enjoying this, as were the jabbering policemen, some distant paramedics, and a woman with a ten year old boy, all of whom making commentary on my deepest, darkest psychologies, and I was handcuffed; so it goes.

Hauled to my feet, and stood there in the middle of the street amidst some ten or twelve cops, my hands cuffed behind my back, I concluded 'visibly' as possible, 'I'm in trouble.' I decided not to resist arrest; that I should go with the whole river of situations here, that I was a criminal, and that I shouldn't cause more of a scene. But perhaps police thrive on that trouble. Perhaps they like a fight? As they mingled about, seemingly anticipating further criminal activity from me, it was as if they did. So when they bundled me into the wagon, saying "Thanks mate," a thousand times each, it was as if my acquiescence to the arrest was something of a disappointment to them. "Thanks mate," "Thanks mate," they went as if I'd upset them. Then I was on my way to the police station. During transit I realised that it's probably not a very good idea for me to have a fight with any black men in the future.

Needless to say, when I was on that 614 that Monday, and the only man to fight was black, I thought twice.

Racism

The frankly staggering three months I lasted in university possessed both a charm, wherein prevalent was our feeling of having made it there, and a dark solitary essence, impressed by that unsaid inability of a social group to sufficiently communicate with itself. I was very much the antihero of the latter feature.

Early on into the semester there was some miniature sort of social change going on. Of course, the same would have happened whether I was part of it or not, but in this case I was, and it was a great deal personally upsetting. It is both difficult and unsatisfactory to describe the change in any explicit way - nevertheless, all it amounted to was, in short, racism.

It hadn't occurred to me, before, that this form of abuse would affect me in any negative way, being that for a long time in my experience it was something I had dealt with. I was able to discuss football with Muslims, physics with Jews, art with Africans – and so on, with any person of any ethnicity. Yet my only experience with the Chinese was limited to quite a nice one back before the period when I was sectioned, and just after the cocaine, and one which admiration and appreciation were exchanged.

One hot July day in Hyde Park, I had been reading some novel while sitting on the grass. On my back I lay with my satchel a pillow. Nearby a threesome of two young blondes, who seemed to be having fun with a kite, and a young man around my age at the time, balding and, apparently, a tad shy of interacting with his companions. Close by, some Iranian family, with a father attempting to control his energetic child of three, were enjoying a day out in the sun. Then midway between these groups some young Chinese tourists gathered to sit on the grass, and absorb English culture amongst themselves.

Some middle-aged short man in a mustard yellow shirt marched vacantly across the lawn. "Complete moron!" I called psychically, and in jocularity, and chuckled to myself and went back to reading. But soon, I became drawn to this threesome playing with a kite.

The girls, well, they were clearly having fun, laughing and yelping like children, and it wasn't for some time of observing the young man sitting in their company, that I recognised that on some surreptitious level, on some playful level, his friends were teasing him.

When I saw that he was withholding an inner desire to join the girls in their game, mingled with a conflict about the reasons why he wasn't able to do that, I saw why they were mocking him. 'If I had two girlfriends like those,' I thought, still watching him quietly from behind my book, 'I would play and laugh, and laugh and play with those girls; and then in the end... they'd sleep with me!' But clever innocence then showed me that, even if the young man was, with all due respect, still sleepy in the day of enlightenment that was this day, still he had friends who were attractive girls. 'Just think,' I dreamed, 'of knowing those women! Just think,' I imagined, 'of going over there to talk to them, all three – what we could learn! What fun we would have!'

It was then I felt a glare. It was coming from my right and its source was the group of Chinese tourists, specifically a couple – a male and a female – who watched me as I considered the threesome. This young and clearly very bright pair (perhaps even intellectuals) seemed to have picked up on my thoughts about the scene, and consequently agreed with me.

We looked at each other in a way that told me we had been thinking the same thing about the same situation, and I smiled to them, and in return I received what was the most peaceful sense of calm serenity. And I felt that if these chaps had to go with a single reassurance, that one person from this part of the world was kind, it was me. The sentiment was interrupted by a further small group of Chinese tourists, who had on rollerblades and tried to walk over the grassy ground, laughing for youth. I saw the groups clock one another; our friends with a certain disappointment. Yet, with a purposeful giggle, the rollerbladers seemed to say 'Some tourists like clever things; *we* like to laugh!' And I saw this surreptitious exchange. Our friends saw that I saw it.

I had gone back to reading my book and then, under the powerful glare they were giving me, I began to feel very big – as though my heart and mind were growing under cultivation. I had never had a feeling like this before; of being completely respected and admired – of being loved – and my only response was that I snatched a look at the two as if to say 'Stop! It's very nice, but I'm not used to it!' They looked away from me then, as a mark of flattery, and I wish I'd have reacted differently, for it was a very nice feeling and I would have liked to have seen where it led.

And that was it. That was my experience with the Chinese. Of course, this was all before antipsychotics, so in fact things were different at university campus.

In fact, I could not have anticipated the damage medication had done to the part of my cortex that could have felt the love just described, such that on several occasions here it was the case I had come to be socially stuck. The whole upset became clear when I found simple requests of particular people working the counter at the university refectory caused abusive reactions.

"Wa you sey?!" she asked, with a cross face, as I stood nonplussed at the situation that was happening now.

"Um," I tried again with a smile. "Can I have a cheese and ham baguette, please?"

"Wasa? Wassa chissy hum babette?"

"No", I returned a third time. "A cheese and ham baguette."

"I don unna stan chissy wa?"

I looked about me in confusion, for assistance. I even pointed at the thing.

"This one, look!" I chirped with a frustrated smile.

"I'M SORRY?!" yelped a woman, who appeared next to me with immediacy (although I could see nothing as to the reason behind her apology, seemingly made to thin air!). Evidently I had become an enemy to the campus.

"Wa you sey?" said the Chinese woman at the counter.

With exasperation, I ruminated quickly, and soon realised I was being too earnest at her misguided protection of interests, which is what it must have been. That is, my hapless happiness under the glare of such obvious provocation was working against me, and I had an idea. I approached the counter one last time and said, in the angriest, most agitated low voice I could, eyebrows furrowed scornfully, "GIVE ME A FUCKING CHEESE AND HAM BAGUETTE NOW!" I thumped the countertop. Of course, it was an act.

In any case, the lady smiled with a strange sort of satisfaction at my outburst and got me my lunch.

So, thought I, all it takes is a little emotion?

The same sort of thing happened later on in the Burger King at the nearby Galleria. The story here, though, did not have a happy ending.

"Hot chocolate milkshake?" said the Asian girl working there.

"No," I tried. "Just a chocolate milkshake."

"Hot chocolate milkshake?" she said once more.

"No!" I whined, with a depression. "Not hot."

"Sorry, we don do hot chocolate milkshake."

"Look, I'm not asking for a hot chocolate milkshake. I just want a chocolate milkshake." I managed not to get angry.

"I don unna stan!"

Oh, not this again. I asked to see the manager, who arrived, an Indian student, and I tried to explain the situation to his good self. Good thing that Indians and Brits have tied up all the loose ends in their relationship.

"So you want a chocolate milkshake?" he asked, with genuine intention to help.

"Look," I said. "Well... no, thanks.... goodbye."

As I walked off I saw that the manager was giving the assistant a dressing down, for losing customers, but I knew she had won this round. I could have done with that drink that day; I was thirsty, and to walk away without it I began to sense that I wasn't the easy going customer I thought myself to be. Something had to change.

Now perhaps it was this particular day, or maybe some other nearby one, that I came to resolve this little problem of institutional racism, in which it seemed apparent that some people knew me better than I knew myself. Of course, what wasn't true was that my evident prejudice was one of an intentional basis; and instead the result of social innocence. However, this innocence did not reflect on the stress and pressure that befell me at the whim of the Chinese.

I was on a bus, of course, when I realised.

I've always considered myself white British. That's what I put on every equal opportunities section on every form I've ever filled where that was necessary. Always have done; always will.

My father, however, is mixed-race Samoan. My mother is Welsh English. I am of a skin colour that, as I was growing up, people would call 'lovely', 'tanned', 'nice', and in summers I would always go a deep tanned colour. White friends would claim to be jealous, it being the case that white skin is unattractive and tanned skin is good. So in that sense I was a happy child.

Except also, although I didn't realise it at the time, my white friends suffered a racial complacency on my part, something unseen in the eyes of children, and which was sort of a mockery of white stupidity. I was assured that I had a 'white' brain, a 'white' mind, and a 'white' outlook. Yet all the while in my complacency there was an undertone of 'something else' of which I did not know. To be fair, I never so much as thought about the white 'race', by which I mean I never saw differences, and in fact (I grew up in the eighties), 'white' was a dirty word. So it seemed. They got a bad press. It was almost racist to be white. You would find new terms such as 'positive discrimination' entering the language.

So growing up I never really had thoughts about the

whites. I suppose the fact that I was disliked by, well, at least two 'true Brits' in my junior school classroom, perhaps sort of compensates. Timothy wasn't a very academic child; *I* was. And we rarely saw eye to eye, other than those times when he had to acquiesce to the fact that his sister was in love with me, and he had to live with this knowledge. If he had been one of the school's bigger children, then I imagine he would have been a bully to me. As it was, for all his schoolboy cheekiness and childish naughtiness, directed many times against myself, his memory remains his saving grace. "You know what, Daniel..." he started, in a classroom at the end of one break time, at a far enough distance that I not be a threat; close enough to make his point. "You're THICK!" he cried with a mean laugh, and his friend Tom laughed warily, as well.

"I'm not thick!" I replied confusedly.

"You're thick!" he went again, and said, "When you was born it was rit on your 'ead, THICK!"

"I'm not thick. Why do you think I'm thick?" I asked, curiously interested, but ready to make a lunge for him.

"You can't think!!"

I gave chase. I was the bigger kid, but Timothy could rely on quickness of pace, being that he was a fast runner. I never caught him. I never did. Timothy was one of the least clever in the class. What did he mean, can't think?

Inevitably, I sat atop the 614 Uno bus going back

through Edgware, thinking all the while about my poor race relations, and I began to consider the legacy of the white folk I saw on the street below.

'Police are mostly white,' I thought, 'and they're arseholes. But really this country is theirs. White people seem so uptight all the time,' I thought. And as I was thinking these thoughts my gaze fell upon a white couple at a crossing. They were looking into the traffic and seemed to view it authoritatively. I mulled deeply for a brief moment, on the sense of protection I had from their presence, and then I realised, "God! White people are cool!" I'd never realised that before. I'd never associated the white person with a capacity for fashion!

So there it was: my first positive conscious thought about white people! And I was only twenty seven! When that dawned upon me, it was like the flood gates of racial ignorance opening up and the reservoir of racial acceptance spilling forth onto the pastures of social tension, extinguishing the fires of social conditioning. I never looked back.

Funnily, after my little epiphany there, I started to see the sense in which whites get a lot of negative attention. I began to see what else I could think about white folk, and at that time it also occurred to me that all the hassle I was having on campus with the Chinese was a direct effect from my heretofore unwitting ignorance against whites. Now that I loved whites, now that I had a reason to love whites, I could love everybody.

However, I also began to notice at that time that

our newly beloved white folk harboured an apologetic attitude within the dynamics of social interaction. What I noticed was, in one way or another, their reaction to the knowledge of their being white. Getting off the bus in Burnt Oak, I noticed this shame in a stranger at the stop. "Hey buddy!" I yelled innately. "You are white!"

The man looked down shamefully, until he heard me say, "And it's cool!" and he was happy.

I repeated the action for nearly every shamefaced white person I saw after that. "Hey, lady!" I shouted to a woman in some distress of sorts, on the next bus. "You're white!" I accused. She started to look downwards in disgust of herself. "But it's cool!" I yelled with a glare. Finally I had some sense of something going on, and how I could be useful on these streets. She seemed settled about that, but she didn't thank me. Why would she? I had just exposed the way she was identified in the world. I felt proud of myself anyway, and having arrived at my stop, alighted and walked away, chest puffed. As the bus pulled off, I heard someone call, "But you're not even white!" I turned, but the bus was gone.

My tongue was jammed up right on the roof of my mouth as I began to recall the white legacy. 'God,' I thought, 'I think I'm beginning to see Hitler's point. God, what did I just say? What's happening to me? But Hitler did have a point though. White supremacy. Oh my God – I am the most racist cunt!'

So it came to be, on that 614 back from Hatfield Business Park, on a brooding December evening, that I encountered the following situation of conflict. I mean, really, I was still stewing about not having lamped that Indian IT student. It wasn't the act I missed out on that caused my frustration, but the fact that he deserved it. And by now my personality had become that of nightclub bouncer – arrogant and self-assured, and hard. There were just four people on that bus today – one was the bus driver and one was a girl of student age, and she was with the third, a young black male student, and they were having a little chat. Someone needed to get it.

I was at the back (lower deck) to the right; the two students a seat in front on the left. Now here it must be said that, though I had anger, aggression to release, and that was inevitable, I never wanted to hurt anybody at all. It was just that the illness or the medication (the former wasn't a question) engendered the perception that all men I encountered wanted a fight. They thought they were harder than me; and if I let them alone they had 'won' already. This feeling persisted, and not all on my part.

And I was a racist now – WHITES RULE!! – so what I did was I locked into a stare upon the back of our black friend's head, and listened in to their conversation. (I was searching for signs of sexist bullying). In fact, the lad wasn't doing too badly in that the female he spoke to seemed most interested in him, his life, his studies and what he had to say. So I sort of left him to it on such a front, although I was having lots of violent inclinations against a brother. The bus lurched past trees and bushes, and as I envisaged punching him from this side, I could swear I almost saw him responding as though really hit. As I fantasised an attack from another angle he seemed to move in that direction. His girlfriend had since disappeared, and as I saw my violence being played out against our friend, it became like a dance – a mad, secret dance between assailant and victim: I punch you; you react – I punch you this way; you react that. It really was a performance of souls; quite uncanny, and served to reinforce a philosophical sense of nature and mind connecting. I bit my tongue. Because if I hit this guy I'm going to get kicked off the bus and we're in the middle of nowhere. "Hey pal," I went aggressively. He looked up at me. "What are you studying?"

"Economics," he said, now with confidence. "You?"

"Philosophy and English," I boasted. "But I've finished my studies."

"Why's that?" asked our friend.

I told him the story of the seminar in which I lost my composure, and went on: "There's too much stress here. I can't go back."

Then, in a flash of youthful cleverness, the young student said, "Maybe it's a case of 'not the right course for you'."

I've always remembered this saying, and while at the time it struck me as pre-emptive of the end of our discussion, it was also bang on the money. Obviously, I had anticipated a somewhat easier ride than the one I got in university. However, I wanted to fight, still, and our student friend had made a phone call. I think he was able to discern that, in fact, I wasn't a very nice guy, probably a little racist, and out to cause trouble. I think he knew I wanted to hit him. In any case, my stop had come, so I stood to leave. 'Shall I hit him?' I asked myself one last time.

'Fuck it, I won't.'

And I got off the bus.

"Fuck yourself," said the lad as I did, probably to the person on the phone, but in a way such that you cannot be too sure. And right there, as the bus pulled away with another failed opportunity at violence going along with it, my frustration surged. A different black guy, standing there at the bus stop, seemed to make himself big in front of me as I walked past. Was it my imagination, or did blacks instinctively know of impending trouble? That is, could they tell when there was a white racist looking for a situation to start? In any case, I took it that they did and walked around the corner where there was another stop. In fact, as hard as I thought I was, as capable of fighting as I felt, as up for a fight as I felt, I was scared, confused and tense.

Festival

Having ridden the 614 UNO bus four times a week for something like thirty miles there and back, and I, already diagnosed mentally ill, plus the fact that it was full every time, and I hate commuting, and most of those commuters were teenagers, added to that the fact that much of this time was spent either having to hold my hands over my ears or in complete deathly silence (both equally as stress producing), after a while, inevitably, it had taken its toll.

As we have seen, this commute plus the stress of university life tried me with all it could to break me. And, at this time, what for you could have been easy but for myself proved only to harness negativity, just culminated in pain that no one deserved, bad vibes like you never felt, violence like in movies, only reality. If you have done your best in life, then you should expect more. Your action goes into a melting pot of effects, and then the free will goes to your brain, and a raincloud comes. You remember days of dancing next to speakers so loud you could see the music. The alternative was to cool off in corridors for health and safety, having come to need smoke.

I was not far from home. The grey streets turned a shade darker as we made our way home, and formulaically at that. The anger of the day was building up in me, and we were running out of time. In fact, time was moving fast, and it was just a short amount of it before we'd have to go to eternity.

It was the case that I had walked these streets before, and on at least one occasion, backwards. That was a recent endeavour in fact, in which it had occurred to me that time is relative to nothing, and it wouldn't make any difference, and nobody would notice anyway.

But never had I ever been as angry before as I had been at this point. The lads had got me beat; I had proved nothing to nobody, and my masculinity had suffered a blow. So really, as I sat seething over the recent circumstances, and in my defence, you could probably forgive me for my next act.

The bus pulled away (it was the 32); the dark night flew with it. I was sat on the left of the bus near the aisle. A man in a navy blue jacket was sat on the right (obviously, he had issues and was beginning to annoy me). It was an ominous feeling that came over me like a night creature, and I hadn't even looked at the fellow's face, and I thought, "Fuck it." And I lamped the poor guy with my elbow. And I grabbed his head and there was fear and surprise in that bus. And someone cried, "CALL THE POLICE!" as I threw the man forward so that his head cracked upon the bus's windscreen, which cracked it. And then he went down.

"CALL THE POLICE!" someone cried.

The bus stopped, and I thought, 'Run'. It had stopped outside the hospital entrance, so I ran through there to the building at the back where they have a mental illness ward: The Dennis Scott Unit. And I ran to the occupational therapy rooms, and I sat there and I smoked a cigarette. That was where I met Benny for the first time.

I still see Benny from time to time; he lives in the area. We sort each other out with cigarettes, but we've hardly even had a chat. I think we once had a five minute conversation: I found out he took economics, hears voices, very clever mind. Big guy. The biggest in town, some would say. He slouches about in jeans that hang down about his arse and has a back-pack and he used to go swimming. Fuck me! He used to swim in Fitness First, but it wasn't really swimming. Now, *I* used to swim – to actually swim. But Benny just went there to walk up and down the lengths. Swimming was sort of an excuse, but mind you, nobody would call it swimming.

Benny was there in the occupational therapy room already, which I approached using the back door, and sat and smoked. If memory serves me I was still feeling very angry and very mad; very crazy. Let me say about this feeling, that it was anger – it unsettled me and felt as though it would never go away – but it was an evil and sickly psychotic sort. Psychotic anger stays there. Psychotic anger is not real – it is not really connected to the world; it is a sort of 'neuro-fibrillary tangle': the product of thought disorder; chemical imbalance. I wonder at the evolutionary purpose of such a phenomenon. Perhaps it is merely a device of biology to make obvious a mental state that's distressing you. Perhaps it is a genuine defect, a side effect of psychosis. But you can still feel it. Something told me it would be wise to avoid talking to Benny.

But he wanted to know which ward I was on: none; what meds I was on: none; did I drive? Yep! I told him I'd just been in a fight. He was more talkative then than he'd ever be again. We didn't come to blows.

I found myself in the square outside. I lay on one of the benches there, needing to calm down, and closed my eyes. My psychotic mind set to search for its natural goal, a removed reason, and found nothing but a darkness of colour. I felt a desire to die; the very reaches of my black unconscious had Fourier transformed and annihilated to a point; my body had calmed, for my anger had focussed on itself, found itself, and realised it had come to an end: the end of consciousness, the end of conscience, my consciousness ebbed away, and I lay with arms across my chest and I slipped away into death; I died. For one second I died. Total conscious collapse, mental blackout. Yet I was still aware and couldn't go all the way.

Yet I was dead, still, and for that moment I lay in

death-stench of eternity, entombed, having a feeling so at peace I could have never awoken. My spirit hung over my body and my brain was empty and it trickled mind-substance into the grave of my heart. I jolted.

And I jolted back into existence with a shock, the light of death having shot right into my soul, as if having been underwater too long. The feeling was beautiful.

And mad as I was I, managed to find my bearings, which took me home by a route perhaps begun from a bus stop before or even after I had alighted. Yes, there was a commotion around this area of Colindale. I was still so angry... still so angry.

****

It's true you have sometimes to think retrospectively. The images in your life, though at the time seem fully dynamic, are actually fixed, with the seat of your consciousness being the frame. This is especially true when under the spell of psychiatric medication. But there was a time when images of recollection would fluidly move, as if fresh to the moment of remembering; although such a notion to a man of my experiences is left to memory, and cast as simply that. Yet I remember it – I can remember fluid life.

The synthetically glimmering green of the hexagon-patterned pasture that seemed thick to the eyesight on this fresh morning in the sunshine; bottles (empty, crushed, plastic) and bags and cigarette butts and flattened beer cups were sporadically squashed on the field's surface, with many footprints pointed in no particular direction. They could only mean one thing!

We are here again.

Yes, that miniature city where moments are made, where one could be forgiven if one wanted to reflect, the seething mass of hundreds and thousands of people walking about in no particular direction, in the empty and desolate moment of a dewy morning amidst an LSD comedown. There are smouldering fires.

Inside a tent, yet so far away from sleep, I listened to the huge piping introduction to Symphony No. 1 in C major by Beethoven on my cassette walkman, and admired my big hands. Maybe I did sleep... The deep green of the fabric of the tent and the sunlight beyond shining in made me feel ever so slightly silly about the hang-ups I'd had persistently in the months prior to this time. I reached for my diary to record the depth in this music.

I thought of what was outside this cocoon: the distant sound of techno and horns, as revellers unwilling to settle down any time soon partied away the morning, and I thought of how they made such good use of their short time here, and I thought of the opportunities – the opportunities! – to be had in a morning such as this, and I opened the zip of my tent to see that world of opportunity streaming into my gaze. There was a moment of fear as I flinched now in a realisation at the sheer size of such a place, and glanced down. I was alone but yet did I hear a voice: it said, "You know what, Dan? – You haven't got the bollocks!" It was all I needed to hear.

October is normally mushroom season but this was July and it was a festival and though I'm really not telling the tale of better times, it is better that we hear how they did even once exist, and usually due to the glory of the effect of a shroom. I was even taking things slowly! Leaving the tent that warm morning having found my bollocks beneath the divine images that came along with that poignant voice, I went for a piss.

On the way down a dry track from the hill I saw my first beauty – a beauty! Without hesitation I approached her and promptly declared, "Oh my God – you're fucking gorgeous!"

She replied with flattered surprise, "Get off!"

I think she liked it; I went in for a kiss. She turned, at the last second, her head and I pecked her cheek.

That day was to embody the idea of what some know as the crux of evolution, in the form of similar experiences as above, except ten, twenty, thirty-fold. For the few too many early morning youths paying off their ticket through work by picking litter were soon to know the energy of one who would play and play and discourse and entertain with such sex appeal it's a wonder I did not get an STD, or kissing disease, or kiss anybody or have any sex.

Herein lies the experience of the talented and famous; those who have the spark to entertain. If the images are confused, or prose too dense, at least please know that there was such deep fluidity in this experience that I will never know again. With lectures and material some might call overt, such that we would all open our hearts to life, and hug and love, and four young guys would even open themselves to that point of coming out as gay there and then, and lion-like purring over the body of named individual Esmeralda, and the girl with the sunglasses and according grin, and Maggie, and the man who came right back to life under my hand, please know – this was Glastonbury 2003....

Fuck it! I'll tell you about it.

So, after going in for that kiss off the beauty, and her having turned her head, and me getting just a cheek, I realised she was waiting for someone who must've been in the loos, and probably her boyfriend. I wanted to ask her if that was true; if she did have a boyfriend. I wanted to tell her that, love, the man does not appreciate you, hence let me take you away from his grasp and we can run off like lovers into the new morning, and laugh and laugh, and be like nymphs of the forest, and let me have you – let us have each other. Please!

Yet I am not as fortunate or as good at planning as that. And so it was with reluctance that I had to move away and on to the possibilities of new pastures. Our dreams died there with the moment, yet in this place, such dreams would regenerate in the manner of a pixelated hero in some computer game – and such was the feeling, and hence context, of the following instances.

A little further down, and for which such a festival is infamous, were more loos. The morning sun was a child peering at you over the bus seat of the hilly horizon. Sparked in mind from the lucidity of the earlier encounter, I had to show restraint, and took a piss in the urinal, and could see the myriad of tents and revellers and rising smoke from where I stood. And when I was done I made my way out, passing a large tattooed and shorn-headed character, and an older man who seemed shy in his elderliness, and wore a green army jacket, who went into the compound. Immediately I was approached to my left by a bearded person whose clothes may or may not have been denim but who had in his hands a small box with a winding handle, which he began to wind, and in a Liverpudlian voice sung this:

"When the day is long and the night is young, and everyone is dancing,

You must be sure to play the tune; the feeling is enchanting,

It won't be long before the song is at the end of flow

And that is when my little friend will come to say 'Hello!'"

And at that point a Jack popped out of the box, and it was all I could do but laugh and laugh. I looked at the man as if to say 'Do you know how funny that was?' Yet the poor man couldn't conceive it, and I imagine he must've thought me mocking him. I had to share this with the world, and I grabbed the next person walking by, still giggling, and said to him, "Mate, you have to see this!" But our friend was overcome with shyness and didn't perform his act.

I moved away in the end, as the Liverpudlian bade me farewell, and I walked on over towards the main stage thinking how cool people are. It was early yet, so there were not the thousands of people making their way about, but there I saw three young chaps, and noticed how cool one of those appeared to look, and I told him. "You look so cool!" I said. The chap was about twenty and wore blue denim jeans and white trainers and a brightly coloured shirt, and he was chuffed as could be! And I was glad that he was chuffed, because I had meant it: he did look cool! The chaps walked off, and although I sensed his two friends may have suffered a little jealousy, the sentiment was there and we'd done our bit, and we went separate ways off into the morning. I revelled in the power of honestly spoken words.

And there, in the shade of the area before the main stage, was a line of bending people with black plastic bags, who appeared to be just starting a morning of picking litter, and the line extended the length of the field. Yet, apparent to me at that time, being that my psilocybin enhanced mind was loud with happy thought, was that these young people were so silent in their work: an anomalous phenomena, given that their brains were essentially capable of so much more. 'Ah, my children,' I thought on approach. 'This will never do!'

"What's all this?" I began, in the inquisition of one young lady. "A funny way to enjoy this festival!"

The young lady murmured something inaudible, as she looked up doe-like from her preoccupation.

"Sorry my love? Speak up a bit!" I said.

"She said she has to do this for her ticket," said the young man who was working beside her. The young lady smiled shyly. There was a photographer taking shots

"What?! Work for a ticket? Surely it's a conspiracy," I continued. "Surely we should all be enjoying the warmth of this wonderful morning with the comfort of a vodka and joint, no?"

The ears of several others had perked up and were beginning to listen in with curiosity.

"I myself was able to procure a ticket without much effort, that is true," I said, deciding to spend a moment in these young people's company. "Yet I had indeed attempted to blag my way in, of course. It is only natural! I came up with a story to tell the person at the main gate, which was that my friends were inside and they had my ticket, and I had no phone to contact them, and I have no money and no way of finding them and I really want to go in, and my girlfriend's in there, and I have to find her and I'm really at a loss. And I started trying to cry, and sort of did cry, so the lady I was talking to seemed to feel pity for me and she said come with me. And she took me to a van and there were some men in hi-viz jackets who said to get in, and I thought Yes! They're taking me in! But then obviously the van drove to the outskirts of the festival and they kicked me out and said don't come back!"

People around me started laughing at this. I glanced about to see that thankfully they appeared to be laughing with me instead of at me, and that was a good feeling. The photographer looked at me harshly.

I continued talking. I was just saying what was on my mind. But now, I wasn't just talking to two or three people. It seemed that I was addressing the entire line of workers, plus anybody who happened to walk by. They were mainly young men and ladies, and everyone seemed engaged in what I said. It was an opportunity I was able to take advantage of. The light of the morning shone down upon us all, and I kept noticing words on a sign that somehow seemed neon. My discourse (for that was what it seemed to be) was borne on the wings of all my experiences of the past year or so, which was a year so full of events that it was easy to joke about them. I was like a comedian, and the main field was my stage, yet my mind was ripe with thought after thought, and I sought to tell them everything.

I began to explain the hidden workings of the recent terror attack in America, and furthermore interposed my lecture with explicit realisations as they occurred to me there and then. The pickers listened happily, and soon I realised their line had become a V-shape with me at the vertex, and I was slowing down their work, so I picked up a bag and began to pick litter with them. That task got boring really quick, so I stopped and walked a bit further up the field.

There were particular characters, I must say, and not just fifty random people: it was a directed speech. The females were each the loveliest sort and my concentration was toward them in the main. In fact, I was horny as hell and much of my behaviour was aimed towards convincing somebody to have sex with me. In fact, my horniness gave rise to a huge image of one particular outcome of this experience: that we get to know each other so well that we might have an orgy here in the field. That soon became the impetus of my discourse. It was becoming hot, so I took off my suede jacket, inside which was a half bottle of vodka and a bag of liberty caps, and lay it on the ground.

I have previously mentioned Esmeralda. Esmeralda wasn't called Esmeralda; I don't know what she was really called. One of my epiphanies as I walked about the field thinking myself some Aristotle or Plato type philosopher was that a woman should be named by her man! I approached this young lady (she had been listening closely to everything I had said). She was a girl of elfin features: her hair was black, her body was slight, she wore blue denim and her eyes were hazel. "A man should name her woman," I claimed, at the closest distance to her. "And I name you..." There was a pause as all the nearest young people listened in. "Esmeralda!" You could visibly see how such a name was a disappointment to all about me, for its inaccurateness, and everybody groaned, including the named individual.

Nevertheless, Esmeralda forgave me. During my speech there, at one point, it had become necessary to see if we were compatible for love by means of a momentary embrace. She ran towards me, arms outstretched, and I reached out for her to receive her, yet at the very last moment there was a rather embarrassing clash in which we sort of banged our heads. I mean, you could tell that poor Esme was upset, but in fact I found it to be quite hilarious and laughed about it for a few seconds. The little pixie continued with her work, and I continued to talk.

I was talking about this, that and the other (all highly relevant and interesting stuff), but in the main I was talking about how we as humans must make it our distinct and necessary duty to truly realise for ourselves what is the meaning of social conditioning. That is, I said, we must be absolutely and utterly true to our very human nature and be as honest as possible about who we are, in order to be free. "If we want to be free," I suggested, "then we must realise that the true state of being has nothing to do with lusting after the members of the opposite sex!"

In any case, at that point I became surrounded by four young men, hardly twenty years of age, who had been listening intently to my fascinating discussion and, deciding they liked the sound of pure freedom, said "Here we are, what do we do next?"

"What," I said as I viewed them with admiration for their bravery in the face of social adversity. "You have understood me? You are coming out?"

The young men shrugged and said, "Sure?"

'Well eat your heart out,' I thought! 'I've assisted these lovely chaps into the light!'

In fact, I had no idea what was supposed to happen next. Like I say, I'm not very good at planning things. I didn't know if it was certain that we had to perhaps embrace; that is to say, kiss! The young chaps were not altogether embarrassed about the situation, but here, I must admit, I fumbled. That is to say, I was not prepared for their honesty, and in retrospect I wish I had been, for I admired them very much. What happened in reality was that I said something in the manner of reversing what I had been talking about the entire time, though what that was I'm not entirely sure, yet it became awkward then, and we all ended up looking at our feet. For I was enamoured with my female audience! (They looked so pretty).

As you can imagine things went on largely in the same vein as this for the rest of the time that our friends the litter pickers of Glastonbury 2003 had to work. By the end of the experience many of us were at the top of the field sitting around on benches and talking. A nice woman asked me how old I was, and because I had recently been thinking about this question, I could answer without hesitation: "I'm 24! How old are you?" The nice lady seemed to momentarily forget how old she was, because she took a moment or two to answer, that she was thirty two! As I spoke to her, however, I sensed there to be a 'draining' of life in the man that was sat to my left. So I turned and I put my hand on his shoulder, and you know, I was right because he seemed to immediately become filled with colour and happiness, and a smile played on his lips.

I was grandiose as fuck, man. I stood up and continued to walk and talk, and some people liked it, and some people didn't (one person was visibly distraught; my speech seeming to hurt his brain). Soon I realised I had forgotten to pick up my jacket, which had my vodka and liberty caps inside, and by that time there were thousands of people walking around and I had no idea where it was – which was a shame: I could have done with some more shrooms. Plus I liked that jacket.

****

What there are are the times. Now, getting back to that strange time of uncanny strength, well... everybody loves their uncles. Education for a year at the college of Harrow, well... that was grand. Before then and after then, well, there are times that I found myself needing to find my mojo, my flow; to get in the zone. Many images have come to my mind, and so, within the process of finding my flow once again, yes, regeneration of that temporary glory of momentary standardisation, by which I mean the realisation of moments in full capacity of the senses, that is, fully woken up from out of that dreamlike time so responsible for the anger and violence of more recent days, I remember a bench – that bench on the side of the small field in the summer of the winter of my frustration, and the stalks of watercolour green and blue-grey pavement, and the true and pure Christian mission of prosaic construction, and wanting there to be God.

We've gone back very far now. I'm in my still grey jumper and leather satchel – yes, I must have looked very studious. I had come to this area to see into signing up to the college here, that I may enter the vestibules of some higher learning establishment. And how pleasant it would be to perch there, at that bench, in the heat of the summer, and think of God and His holy word, and think how lost I once was, within the pinnacle of His visitation. What was that look, just now occasioned in my direction, from the eye of some youthful nymph of the summer of this particular field?

It was by the road, and cars would shoot past, up toward the top of the hill, yet their humming did not distract me enough from the glances that were shot me by the lad with his summer beer, and shorts and Hacket tee. The station behind me spilled the ants of Harrow's hill and the clouded yet hot sky let out answers to the questions of a misguided and troubled outpatient as I, within the confines of a recreational field by a road which went up the hill, tried to talk to God.

The students, well, there were twelve or thirteen hanging around; lazing, in fact – relaxing: perhaps just out of some seminar or lesson in the college grounds, both males and females, perhaps exchange students. I may have overheard a couple of phrases in the language of German; thus I took them as German. Indeed, they looked German.

It was a time, let me explain, that I can recall, with

the benefit of hindsight, a feeling of loss, and for general conduct I would take my cues from any sign I trusted. As I looked longingly for the love of God in the hot sky, I realised at once a once intuitive but now, shall we say, 'manually achieved' method of hearing Him. And in my mind I heard Him call, to me on this park bench, saying, "I am an idiot!"

With slight but noticeable joy, I noticed the mood of the park change – the German students boring into me; I myself wondering what they had seen. Perhaps they had thought of me as an idiot, having read my thoughts. Yet there in the middle of the field, they each, the twelve or thirteen German students, glared and stared in my direction. Such behaviour is perplexing enough, and I wondered what would be my response.

In my head I saw the scene: an approach, bravado, the raring up and the attack. However, as a man of religious leanings, I would desire to leave the park. And I remember, for some reason, a litter bin being a marker to determine my following actions. Yet thoughtless and desiring instruction I searched the eyes of the beery Hacket-tee lad, and the eyes of the nymph-like beauty, for my next course of action. Both beauties said the same thing in their own way: You must fight.

And I tried, I tried everything I could to pull away from the scene, to avoid confrontation. The consciousness of a thoughtless fool such as I wrangles with these decisions, and I saw that, as I moved to leave, the air would darken in disappointment; the very atmosphere would become saturated with regret; the very strength of the magnetic pull of the humidity of day would not allow me to leave. Everything inside me wished to leave. The compulsion, however, could not be wished away, and confidence and relief filled me whenever I acquiesced in nature's whim. When I moved back into the park and closer toward the students, who had glared and stared, perhaps the Hacket-tee lad and nymph-like beauty were satisfied, for they were happier and smiled, and I felt big. Without great certainty or sureness of myself, I skipped and hopped in the direction of our aggressors. I slid and sidled and I stepped to the centre of the field where they were, these German exchange students, and, glancing at the nymph-like beauty, was recipient to an appreciative smile in anticipation. I think of her now as a sisterly youth bathing in the sun. "Hello," said I to the group, some of which said hi in return.

I remember animatedly booting one of the bigger boys in the head, at which the group excitedly scattered – the females running very quickly toward the station, and a handful of the males jumped up to protect themselves. Another male faced me, from four feet distance.

"Vas da problem?!" he shouted.

"Vas da problem?!" I mimicked, and kicked him in the chest, and the group dispersed. Turning around I saw a younger male behind me, rooted to the spot. I knew the feeling. Yet, I motioned an attack with my shoulders and fists, to scare him, and he shot off. I walked them out of the park.

Glancing once more at the nymph, she shot me a cheeky smiled that seemed to say, "I am a one!"

Then I saw some of the females of the group talking to an official to whom I was pointed out. My original intentions of finding a path through the station were changed, and I had to run the other way; I did not wish to be sectioned again. So I ran down towards the traffic and, deciding to hide, found a car park where I plotted in behind a Mercedes.

In fact, now recalling the memory, I believe I found a door, beforehand, and went to hide through it at a ledge that looked into an office, but a security guard told me to move on.

Then I found my spot behind the Mercedes.

It was not the greatest hiding place, for ten minutes later two policemen came into the car park and, searching under the cars, found me and called me out. "You just beat up some people," the first one said.

"They were being racist!" I reasoned.

"They were white," retorted the policeman.

"They were German!" I replied.

This one spoke into his walky-talky and I envisioned the police-wagon pulling round and taking me away to some cell, and then hospital, and I shook my head exasperatedly at the inevitability of the situation. But the policeman said, "Okay, call the police in, we've found him."

It was then that I realised these men were security guards and not police at all. I saw a gap in the concrete structure by which escape could be made and, having clocked their powerless position, ran toward it and jumped through it. "Let him go," said the second security guard, as I ran away.

In fact, I only ran down a residential road but certainly did find a good hiding place behind a wheelie bin, in the garden of a house. It was true; I had got away.

I was hiding in there, in that doorway of a random garden, for several hours. There had been fear of being caught: after twenty minutes in this place I became aware of policemen searching the area, and using words to coax me out. "We know where you are!" they had said. I'd taken my chances and remained in my hiding spot. I had no intention of going back to hospital.

After half an hour I could hear police sirens going round the area. The feeling of fear gradually intensified and then struck me violently as the sound closely passed where I hid.

Luckily I had my satchel, and inside, my mobile phone on which I called my best friend. He would come after some time, when I was sure the 'search party' had done searching, to collect me and take me home.

Before

Before introduction to the psychiatric hospital, before the onset of full-blown psychosis, before the final hit of coke that brought me to mental illness, and before my religious experience, there had always been a struggle. At times it would be in battle, with others or with myself, or with lovers, and in love.

I have not, since 2001, had a relationship. And only two long term ones up to that time. There were other girlfriends, of course – Danielle, Victoria, Jenny, Karen – but the two most serious partnerships were Kelly and Judy.

Kelly I had liked ever since she came school on mufti-day in full leather. She would walk the same school route as I did, and she walked fast and it was hard to keep up. Many of the students thought she was a lesbian, but I didn't care. I buzzed whenever I saw her, and in the last year, struggled to think of ways to meet her. I feared that school would end and I would never get a chance to meet her and never see her again.

It was probably not the most romantic way to go

about an introduction, but I had told my best friend Gary that I liked her, and on a sunny Friday after school we followed after her, and Gary caught up with her and told her about me.

Kelly is a happy looking blonde, with Irish family, and highly intelligent. Slightly freckled, and cuddly and cute, her taste in music was very similar to mine. Back then it was all about grunge. Kelly was older than me by a year. There was something about her I found intriguing. She was strong and interesting and different. There was no other girl in school quite like her. It being the nineties, and me being in a rock band, I wanted a rock-chick girlfriend – a Courtney Love to my Kurt Cobain. She was perfect.

She arranged with Gary that we should all go to a club; there was an indie one in town, and we went. She would bring two friends. I think that night Gary and I drank a bottle of vodka before meeting Kelly and friends at her place. We may have smoked a spliff. We staggered down Lawrence Gardens cheering and singing. I think one of Kelly's friends tried to come on to me.

In town we got to the club, LA2, on Charing Cross Road. I drank beer, Kelly drank wine. We danced, Kelly and I, to some mix of indie pop and grunge. I do not recall what happened to Gary that night. But we danced, Kelly and I, perhaps to Pulp, or Nirvana, perhaps to Suede, or Smashing Pumpkins; we danced and got close. We kissed for the first time on the dance floor. I remember her arms around me and mine around her. Soon she would take me to a booth and sit astride me, and we made out there for the rest of the night.

I lost my virginity to Kelly. A group of us – her friends and mine – would march to the woods where we would make a fire, and smoke and drink. We'd spent time getting to know each other intimately. We'd kiss and get stoned and play with one another in her bed, to the romantic sounds of Leonard Cohen, and the Doors, and Nirvana Unplugged in New York. We had explored each other, and were close. But our first sexual encounter was, to be honest, hardly romantic.

In the woods by the fire, with twenty or twenty five of us, all drunk and stoned, I was drunk enough and cheeky enough to finally proposition Kelly. "Can we have sex?!" I remember calling over the heads of others.

"Yes!" she'd said. We walked off into the darkness.

It was not romantic in the classical sense, but there *was* a drunken romance to the experience. I remember kissing and playing around with her, and eventually putting on the condom, and finding my way inside her very wet vagina, and making perhaps five strokes before ejaculating and apologising.

I hear that many times when people lose their virginity are awkward, and I felt deeply embarrassed by mine. I explained this to Kelly later, but she alleviated my fears by saying it was okay because the first time is like a barrier, and now we're past the barrier we could do it all the time! I breathed a sigh of relief.

And we did do it all the time, and things improved.

We did it in parks, on the side of ponds, on a wooden horse once. We did it on alcohol, on weed, on LSD, on ecstasy. The time on ecstasy was particularly good. We generally couldn't keep our hands off each other.

Yes, there were many good times, and much romance and passion. There were difficult times too, of course. I pushed her down once, onto the grass, for some reason that had made me very upset. She fell over, and I picked her up and apologised and apologised, and she said it was okay because it showed passion. But I never truly forgave myself for that. She said it showed I cared.

We split, in the end, on amicable terms. I guess that we'd both been feeling at a loss in our relationship; perhaps bored by it. We still enjoyed sex though, and one day we just decided to make love one more time and call it a day. We stayed friends.

I was seventeen by the end of that relationship. I possessed ineptitude at finding girlfriends afterwards, and because of that, for two years I was alone.

During that time I was mostly concentrating on my band Two Five Burn, a grunge rock outfit. We played, when we could, at some cool places on the scene: The Dublin Castle, The Bull and Gate, Upstairs at the Garage. Having recorded some demos and finding our sound, and becoming tighter as a group (which was our fundamental goal), eventually we got some label interest. The stories are different from each band member, but what a fucked up time.

We'd written a song, Sunrize, about this trippy pill

that was going round at that time. One night I'd started the trip with a view to transferring the feeling of trippy pills to everybody else, and also to make anyone on a 'sunrize' feel like we were speaking directly to them. We had had a gig coming up and a desire to play the song at it. Reggie and Alan, guitarist and bassist respectively, never did hard drugs like sunrizes, but Mark, our drummer, did. I think I realised how difficult it is to write music on class A's that night because at that time we found ourselves certainly going round in circles.

My bedroom was the arena for creation; we'd retired there late in the evening, Mark and I buzzing and tripping away, and Alan and Reggie lazing about. The keenness of attitude towards writing the song was matched, oddly so, with the stringent constraints of our ability to connect, Mark and I, due to the heady nature of the trip. We had a conflict between pushing the song forward and wanting to just skin up joints and lie about. The impetus of the night was that we had to get the song ready for the gig, but it wasn't happening, and it went nowhere, and the irony of the song is that our trip that night sucked. All we did was skin up then play a few chords, get stuck, then skin up again. That night drugs and rock 'n' roll certainly were not friends. When you take drugs and do them a lot every drug is an experience – moral, spiritual, educational. Some people made university their experience – for Mark and I it was our lifestyle choice to be on drugs. But that night nothing really happened. God knows how we ever wrote Sunrize, but we forfeited its being played at the next gig.

It was a very turbulent time then. As I said, we nearly got signed – at least, we nearly signed a deal with an independent label. I mean, when you're young and you want to get signed you'll sign almost anything. It wasn't even a label really; just a company that said they'd put our music out there. In any case we didn't sign with them. At the very moment of putting our signature on the dotted line we had a disagreement. Alan and Reggie were good lads – they signed and said with complete honesty what songs they'd had a part in writing. Mark and I had a disagreement; obviously some discrepancy about who had written what song and the rest of it. Basically, he thought he'd written part of this song called Mission, which now looking back he probably did – if I squint and remember there could possibly have been a tiny bit of input that he made on a summer's day in a garden while we smoked cigarettes and jammed on acoustic. In any case now looking back I wish I had have simply given in to our drummer's requirements, said "yes, you wrote that!" and signed the deal. I think we would have given forty percent away, we didn't sign it anyway. If we did, things might have been different.

Reggie uncovered our last written song a short while ago while listening back to mini-disc recordings he'd made of our rehearsals; in particular, our final rehearsal. We were so fucked up back then. It fills me with a sense of resentment to say that in the last days we were so damaged as a band that certain divisions were created between us. I remember sessions in which Alan and Mark would go off and do their own jams, in the manner of rebellion against myself, because they didn't want to become "Dan's backing band". But our last song was such a banger it guts me to hear it. Perhaps the simplicity of the song was such that certain procrastinations developed in our collective mind as to make us all a tad complacent in our work. The day of our final rehearsal we drove back from Holloway to Mill Hill, and on the drive played back the tune from our jam – it was called Get It From You. I had a feeling of a sense of what a brilliant thing we'd made and showing my joy, and then wondering why nobody else was into it. As I say, after all our competence as musicians, we were complacent. That was a very turbulent time.

I remember: Mark's ears stank! It really was quite bad. An ear infection had caused that smell and it made us all sick – a pungent, strong, ear-waxy whiff that often left me leaning out of the van window on route to work, Mark sitting there clueless in the back. He ruined a fair few pairs of decent headphones, I can tell you. Poor old Mark!

We were best mates for a long time, Mark and I. When I discovered his talent for drumming, at school aged fourteen, we found a shared passion for song-writing. We would get stoned in my room of Saturdays and come up with these terrific tunes and words. This one time we hit a harmony, that was so deep and thrilling, that old

Mark nearly shat himself! I mean seriously – we hit the note, which we'd never heard before, looked at one another like have you ever heard anything like this? – and old Mark recoiled in a strange shock of what must have been utter terror! "Whoa!" he went, then had to breathe deeply to regain composure. We recorded that harmony; we used to record stuff all the time. But what a harmony! Some kind of choral freakishness from heaven or hell, it was! We were stoned, but we had something.

We worked on a building site, under the governance of my father, for many years. Everyone who met Mark loved him and remembers him fondly to this day, for his character; he was after all a drummer. A lot of people probably thought of his character better than they did mine. Me, I was a pushy, arrogant little fucker at age sixteen. Controlling. I admit now I wanted to control Mark. My old man, Fred, he decided to become our manager one day. It was a decision I wasn't best happy with at first, it being grunge music that we played, and grunge was all teenage angst and rebellion against authority. I didn't say it to dad, but I wanted control of Two Five Burn. In any case, dad became our manager, and did a great job of it too. He found us gigs and got us to record our music professionally. He had faith in us and recognised we had some talent. Dad pretty much saw every gig we ever played. And mum came along too sometimes. In fact the last gig we ever played, The Vulture's Perch in 1998, there were only four people in the audience who'd come to see us: a chap called Ron, a young lady called Sarah, and mum and dad.

"Hello mum, hello dad!" I remember saying into the microphone.

"Hello Dan!" they called back with a wave.

We played some good gigs, and some bad gigs, and some God awful gigs in our time. The worst, I think, was Upstairs at the Garage, one of the times. I was a little bit drunk and probably stoned as well. On arrival, we'd met another of the bands who'd come up and were friendly to us, and we'd had a drink. Downstairs at the "main" Garage was the group NOFX, which we found to be very cool – we were practically on the same bill as a well known band that had played Reading and stuff. As much of a boost as it was, we played so badly that night – nothing we could do could make it sound good. Quite a lot of our friends turned up to that one, jeering in the crowd as we fucked up song after song. We weren't usually this bad but tonight nothing worked. After the show, backstage, normally the other bands come over to you and say what a great gig you just played. Backstage afterwards this time the other bands looked at us as if to say, "That was so shit!" They didn't even have to say it. They just looked at us as if to say, "So shit!" And they were so right I just looked at them helplessly as if to say, "I know it!"

I could often be a bit of a dick up there onstage. I once had this little idea of doing this dance move with my feet – sort of a jump followed by twinkle toes! I always had these silly ideas. In school, when we played at assembly, my little idea was to let the guitar drop down gradually until the neck was near my face. And I did it – like no one saw! Then onstage later on in years I did this little twinkle toes jump – like no one saw! But I don't think anyone did notice. I didn't have the best stage moves. I'm not Kurt Cobain.

Once at the Dublin Castle gig in '97 halfway through the gig I decided to say, "I'm a builder and I've got builder's hands, and you ain't done a day's work in yer life, yer scroungin'...." Only one person laughed – mum's best mate Carrie. But she did piss herself! Actually I could be pretty funny up there onstage at times. At the Orange in Islington during our set someone called out, "Do you take requests?" and I said, "Only if they're our songs!"

At our first ever gig in Seven Sisters we were about to do a cover version of Sweet Child of Mine by Guns and Roses, and I said, "This one's an oldie... cause we're only little!"

At the Bull and Gate, when this dude wanted to become our manager, and came along to see us, he'd told me that from hearing our tapes he'd thought I was smaller. So when I was up there onstage I said, "I'm sorry if I appear somewhat plump this evening, it's just that I've had four pies!" Being a frontman was a laugh.

We played good gigs and bad gigs, as I say. But I think the best gig we played was at the Bull and Gate one of the times. Mum and dad had gone on holiday. We would never get that many people showing up to see us normally. However, for some reason, this night the venue was packed – there must have been a hundred people! But I think, because normally old man Freddie would be there at the back watching (he had to be, most times, as a chaperone), I couldn't normally fully relax. Tonight though was a real release, like having a free house, which my sister and I actually did that night. I feel quite bad that old Fred would never see the best of me up there onstage. It was hard to share something so personal with him. I feel guilty because he's my dad, and though he did the bollocks, and was a great manager, I wanted to be independent – to have something of my own. What a release that gig was.

****

Well, there are indeed good times and bad times, bad times and much fucking worse times. Two Five Burn fell apart slightly before the millennium; we were so stressed and mad. We all felt that was a massive shame, and after a while I began doing more drugs, which I'd imagined I would have stopped. It got to the point where I didn't know what I was doing, but it couldn't be controlled: Love got in the way.

Relationships are painful. We all know that. There were elements of my one with Kelly that hurt terribly deeply. But nothing could prepare me for the time that came with knowing Judy.

I never knew how much I loved her until many years after we split, but when I look back, even knowing that

I didn't know how much I loved her at the time, when I look back I love her more than ever.

Two years had passed without me being in a relationship, and my group of friends still hung out in the park, some of us taking ecstasy which had become new to us. Two young ladies, Kat and Judy, felt they had the need to be on ecstasy too, to be in our group. I mean, not all of us took the stuff. It was me and Gary mostly who did. The day came when Kat and Judy arrived in the field and said they were on ecstasy. It turned out they both liked to get high on this pill; the pair were mad. In any case we took them both in our group.

We were in the back of Mill Hill park's field and all on pills. Some police in plain clothes showed up in this little ford fiesta van and said they were only there to see that everything was okay; that we were fine and safe. And we milled about on a bench, and I remember Gary being there, and Judy and Kat and me speaking to these "officers", one who was a woman and the other a young man. And during their visit there was talk of a flag, but I knew Judy was making it clear she was fucked, and that's what the officers wanted to know. I said something really witty: it was about a flag; Judy said, in her energetic confusion, "What's a flag?" and I said, "It's a bottle you keep your drink in!" and that was funny to everyone, but I forget why exactly – probably because a flag is not a bottle you keep drink in. But I was going on about a 'flagon', which is. The officers soon got to realise we were okay, but it was obvious we were fucked. Then, as the police got back in their van, they switched on the radio and blared out this house music, and I knew that we would be caught for being high; the girls started dancing, the idiots! I said after, "Those police wanted to check if were on pills and you just proved it to them." And we all laughed at the truth of it.

Judy and I were together. I have so many memories of her; she really was a fun person, she still is I hear. She loved me. It was like a kind of obsession with her. We'd get stoned of a night and the in morning I'd go to work as a labourer, and she would write me these love letters and leave them there on the desk for when I got home, and she left joints with them. She worked on Shaftesbury Avenue at the musical Cats, and started about midday and didn't stop till ten in the evening. Her dream was to be in the show as a performer – I think she does things like that now, if I'm right. But in the evenings on the weekends we'd just take drugs – we'd take class A's and hash – hash was our smoke of choice. It was good to get high. I'm off everything now.

Judy would love to talk. Man, she loved to talk. But back then, when I was a teenager, I was generally a shy person and didn't say much (but they tell me that when I did, people listened to me).

We did a lot of drugs. At Glastonbury we bought about twenty pills and, man, we had a great day when we came down. She tells me that she couldn't stop thinking about me and Kelly having sex. Judy was 'on' too, so... Somebody walked past the tent we were in and was singing, "Nothing ever lasts forever" by Echo and the Bunnymen. We were having a bad argument.

Once, I wrote in my diary:

"In the distance,

Amidst the booming noise,

You search for the heart,

And the yells of joy,

Amidst the cheering and the noise,

At the centre,

You will find me."

That's it. That's how I saw Glastonbury. It was me, all the time dancing and cheering and having an amazing time, dancing hard with cheering ravers all cheering, and once, the DJ/MC noticed we were zoning out – "Come on people make some noise!" he goes... No one was going to cheer, I knew it. It was the last chance for Glastonbury in the midst of hard house, and I knew they were all too self-conscious; they were never going to cheer. But I was stood at a safe enough distance and I knew I had to call something out – the sanctity of rave relied on it. So without hesitation, and just at the right moment, I yelled "OI OI!!" real loud like, and it was a brilliant rush when the whole crowd of hundreds of ravers cheered back at my calls, and the rave was saved.

I was just a kid.

Judy, she fucked off with Tony, this guy she obviously fancied. Sarah was with Mitch at this time; I knew, back at base, they'd ask me where Judy was, and I knew I wouldn't answer. And they did ask that, and I didn't answer; I just shut up. It was a bit awkward. I always remember the awkward moments. The bane of existence is an awkward moment. But being able to get out was always a very good virtue.

I tripped at Glastonbury, and it wasn't bad, but it was weird. As I sat watching the burning ashes of a fire in the early morning on the hill, I remembered what Mitch has asked me about the trip.

"How are the visuals?" he said, with wisdom. And I thought for a second.

"I don't know about the visuals," I responded. "But I like that question!"

Looking back, I can say that I wondered, and remember wondering, 'Am I alright? Is this okay?' But tripping is madness. You forget tripping is not just all about seeing shit. It's a mind thing too, and you need to control it. You get addicted to trying to solve it. Some acid I loved, but most was not that good – 'freaky' is the word. I've had sex two times on acid: once with Kelly, and once with Judy. They were both good fun in their own way.

So we had some nice experiences, me and Judy. In its own way, even the day we split up was nice, but then there were a few weeks of difficulty before it. It was totally confusing really. She would talk and talk on drugs, and once, on ecstasy, we were lying in bed, and she was saying I love you, I love you, I love you, and being on drugs too and perhaps not fully with it I got paranoid she was not being honest. But she was, and she was really upset, and also I was paranoid and probably brain damaged in some way, so... when I said I didn't believe her she was not best pleased about it, I can tell you.

Judy and I split up to the tunes of Beck in her bedroom, and weren't connecting, and we knew we weren't the one. We cried from being out of sync. Someone said I didn't love her, and maybe that's because I found it difficult to show my emotions. But I loved her dearly.

Relapsing

It's hard to think of what exactly it was which caused me to become mentally ill. I suspect it was the drug misuse but even that's not so clear now, ironically. The other night I was asleep, and it was as if I was awake, and I have to take medication. There's this antipsychotic medicine that was given to me, which became quite nice to take, but the day I first took it, it fucked my brain something chronic. That was really bad. But it's an old story that makes me tired of talking, and although it is pivotal, I think I'll leave it for later. I want to talk about what happened to me the other day.

I've recently quit smoking weed – well, for about ten months. Being on it for the most part of my adult life, it's no wonder I have to adjust. Sleeping less and exercising and even working more are the inevitable results of this. I like the feeling. It's strange because I feel higher now than I ever used to do on weed. And not sleeping at night is a good catalyst for psychotic madness. This is such that on some mornings, when the day dawns on the town I live in, I like to generate my gait toward the local coffee shops nearby. This involves, in the one instance, a short walk or even shorter bus journey, during which the place that is the given world around me seems like it's a computer game all the time. And I've clocked it. I've clocked, in actuality, that I'm a fucking lunatic.

The other morning after another sleepless night I go out and start giving it all the mouth – to people, to cars, to passing buses, to mums, to dads. Dancing down roads and stuff. Crossed the A41 at Mill Hill Circus, put my hands over my eyes and walked like a blind man searching in the dark. Traffic allowed me to cross. They even smiled (when I peeked). A bus full of passengers passed by, and I spread out my arms lovingly, as a child tells his mother how much he loves her – THIS MUCH!! How mad? And to the muzzies I blew kisses! To children I danced and called out songs. To Jews, why I saluted and stamped in a regimental way! It was atrocious and brilliant in a badly funny way, and I was in control of my madmen who waited like firemen in the cack of my devilled egg stare.

The rules were obvious ones: when a song drops on the iPhone that rocks the universe, like a mother of a bitch called Max, you dance, dance, dance with the banging of your head and the pretend air guitar – banging like your name was Dave and you like the Wildhearts. Yeah, that was me.

Sadly, nobody expressed any interest in the antics of Toby Anstis, but they did express it with me. The bus stop near Fratelli's wanted to be inside my head. There was food thrown at me, and at that point I knew I had to have a coffee. Lily gave me a free coke, at the shop.

People... now, people remember things. Lily said I'd been unwell. I explained how at times I spend too much life inside, so getting all freaky with the world is inevitable. Unavoidable.

People... people are known to be moody at the worst of times. It can go several ways if somebody can see what's coming to them. If it's a case of someone thinking you are not pulling your weight, then they might talk. Or if someone thinks you're trying too hard, then they might look at you as a joker. You don't want that, so you stop trying to please. And then someone – a builder or accountant walking there (actually, builders are generally alright, and you can't fault your accountants) – might tend to take the piss somewhat in an interesting way. But I find the Jehovah's witnesses to be the most irredeemably lovely people. The dear fellows.

Take, for example, the other day. I spoke to two Jehovah's witnesses, their names to be Tina and Rose, and very nice, I'm sure. Their gift was of the kindest: a pamphlet which I was able to finish in under ten minutes. It did indeed contain some thoughts about the phenomena current to the time of publishing. The Watchhouse is indeed connected to the Jehovah's Witnesses. But, singularly I must say, I went over to have a chat with Rose. Tina had fucked off. And talking to Rose was the best thing, because she was as lovely as a rose. And I swear it was to be an occurrence better than talking to God or watching American sitcoms. She basically talked to me for about half an hour, face to face – no sexual thoughts whatsoever – just pure discourse, lovely discourse of loveliness, for about half an hour about the happiness of her soul, the singularity of being, the truth of the word of God, loads of things. Half an hour. Just her voice, her face and her thinking her thoughts. Nobody I know can be bothered to do that. Had I been a less caring bastard I would've properly lamped her. Not to say I'm a violent sort. I am a sort though. But Rose could be bothered. It was nice. I thought, 'I want to get some more of that.' So I got myself invited up to Kingdom Hall near the Ridgeway. In fact I phoned up my old mate Keith, whom I was having bible studies with a few years ago, and asked him to invite me to the other one – the other Kingdom Hall in Graeme Park. I'm going up there today at two o'clock.

So, I might be a Jehovah's Witness, then. Other people say not to bother. But here, in this day and age, on such a planet as this, there is religion whether we want it or not. And if you're a Buddhist you're a Buddhist; if you're Jewish you're Jewish; if you're a witness you're a witness. Witnessing exists, and it's there and it's not false. I daresay no religion is false, even Islam, although they've got it wrong; it is what it is. From a personal perspective, if God exists (and He does exist) then everyone has a purpose; everyone has a role to play; every thorn has its rose.

It's a system, the world – a system of things, as it

says in the bible. The bible is not called the good book for nothing: it really is a good book. It's tops! I read it the other morning from start to finish within half an hour, not really taking anything in, but really enjoying the word of God. He probably did write the bible, the Heavenly Father, in his own way. I mean, it's the truth to say that it's a circular book in the sense of its eternal language. You can read it from any time of day, any time whatsoever, anywhere, and it will always be a different book. And it is insightful. Without knowing the order of books within the book, I asked God, Jehovah God, to please put my name in there somewhere. I basically turned the page (true story) and it was the book of Daniel. True story.

So yeah, I'm mentally ill. To say things like 'I'm talking to God' or 'I've met God' – met God! – is the sort of thing that gets me sectioned. But if God didn't want me to say it, then I wouldn't have said it. I'm totally open to the idea that I'm having a conversation with the big man.

I'm not.

I'm lecturing the Lord. Either that or God is writing. I don't care – I'm telling the truth. That's not the point. It's hard to understand. It's hard when you think you're a genius. Tomorrow it will be different.

I'm mentally ill. I usually say 'mad' to put a friendly twist on things. But it's not friendly. Well, it is and it isn't. There have been a few uncouth things that I've done. I used to live in Colindale, North London, but I was evicted for having a wank in the communal garden at midnight in full view of the neighbours. I didn't mean anything by it. I'm just a terrible person. It wasn't until that time that I realised what a cunt I am. I mean, it was about eleven o'clock at night on a Thursday. I was drunk on Jack Daniel's. I felt dead inside. I'd bought the drink, I'd fucked it right up by this point in life, and I'd had no friends. Hadn't had a fuck in ten years. As I walked up to my front door I thought 'I'm gonna have a wank in the garden.' I got drunk. Went outside. I thought it was about four in the morning. Took out the old dickens and rubbed myself on the metal fence. Paranoid about if anyone was watching I looked around. I remember thinking, 'I want to get caught'. The thought just popped in my head. I looked around. Up to the flats around. Fuck me, there was a girl looking at me must've been ten. I realised what I was doing, shit myself and ran inside.

Don't worry there was loads of grief about it. Some of the neighbours also saw, and that morning the police turned up at my door. It wasn't a pleasant night's wait; I knew it was coming. Never felt so shit in all my life. What the fuck have I done?

Anyway, went to a prison cell, trapped for obvious reasons. Tried to get out of it. Lied my arse off. Said they made it up because they hate me. Totally denied it.

The neighbours got a petition signed against me with fifty fucking signatures trying to get me kicked out. They said I was a paedophile. I'd never fuck a child. I'd fuck someone who did though. So I was evicted from there.

I'm mentally ill. That's a fucking understatement. I don't know what the fuck is going on. I don't know if I'm alive or gay or dead or genius or God or married or dead or in space or a cunt or bald or fit or gay or strong or Jesus or Mohammed or Buddha or a prick or a twat or a nice man or old or if I want to kill or kiss or if I'm blind or gay or dead or in heaven or shit or worse or angry or clever or good or gay or a wanker or if I wank horses or if I'm in hell or a genius or a twat...

Actually I am all of these things. Every single last one of them. One thing I know. I'm mentally ill. That's a fucking understatement.

Last night I closed my eyes for two seconds – well, two minutes – and time shrunk, and I heard this fuck off huge big bang in my head. Massive, it was. Biggest fucking bang I've ever heard. Shit myself too! I know why it happened as well. God wanted me the fuck to work. How lovely. And He doesn't care what work I do, be it drawing, writing, cleaning or piano playing. He gets the hump with that though; he gets bored playing piano. But just as long as I'm busy writing on Facebook or here or there or drawing on my iPad (which I thank you for Lord; you're pretty sweet)...

And anyway, talking about God: it's all bullshit anyway. You know the world is actually electric. There's no soul. It's pretty unfair really. You grow up thinking there's a soul. You understand the soul. You get it; you see it. But eventually you find out that it's all electric. It's artificial intelligence! These Apple iPads and iPhones, they're all alive!! It's artificial intelligence. The fucking things can think! It's funny. There's no scientists working up there in the iCloud. No one made the iPads and iPhones. It's electric. And it's hell. I know. I been there; I know. It's alright though; you'd like it. You can't not do nothing. You can do what you want. But you want to work and all your friends are there. It's not heaven though, it's hell.

Psychosis

I'm gay. You're there. I'll probably change my mind though, tomorrow. I like this, doing things I do. I like it. I'm gay for the world!! Being gay for the world is good; you have to be. When you're God you have to be. I'm God. God is gay. They reckon God is bald. I'm bald. I'm a bald gay. In the mirror I look bald because I've got no hair, but I'm dead. That's totally shit but not as shit as the fact that I'm fat too. I cannot lose weight. I'm the fattest fuck. I'm not allowed to look good. God doesn't want me to.

Building

I wish to point out that at the turn of the millennium I wasn't having a very good time. From an outside point of view, what with all the drugs going round – me on drugs, clubbing, parties – it might have seemed like I was having the time of my life. But then, it was a very confusing time, socially. There was tension; such tension you could feel it. The entire population of London youth, and probably the youth of the population of the entire country, were on drugs. It started to not be fun anymore, but everyone was addicted, everyone had failed in life, everyone was lost. The scene we saw in our head, the image of a party we saw in our mind, was in direct contradiction to the limitations of the physical world that many had lost connection with and could no longer control. So parties like the 2001 New Year celebrations at the Millennium Dome that had held so much promise failed miserably – misery was the way it could only have gone. Thousands upon thousands of frankly disaffected, unhappy, dissatisfied Londoners hating each other in the illusion of "Having it large". I thought it would "go off" that night. But nothing went off.

Certain saviours of the time were able to give us the hope enough to pull through. Although American rock music, still mourning in the wake of the alternative rock scene, had seemed to be struggling to keep afloat, there were lights in the dark, somehow illuminated by the cause of their own talent, who were not connected to the death of music, who didn't care about that dream of fame and only loved to play. I remember Pearl Jam at Wembley 2001. I remember Beck at Brixton Academy. Two lights, two talents. And as much as their music would carry torches for the genuine, there was other stuff going on closer to home.

I had a job then, on a millionaire's building site, where my dad was the foreman. Actually there were several sites in the Hampstead area. I'd been in the game since leaving school, not through a conscious choice, more through default, yet I could earn money. But it wasn't really what I wanted to do.

Yet the saving grace of having a job where you have to slog your guts off from seven until five, be it digging foundations, carrying barrows of sand, or bricks, or laying blocks, or plastering and rendering, the saving grace was the different sorts of characters you met.

Ideally, I would have preferred to have gone to college and university. You can have your education and parties and you'll likely find a half decent job at the end. Mainly you just learn about your subject. But when Alan, a wiry and lean labourer in his forties who wore a woolly hat, told me that "Farting is good because it scratches your piles," I knew I'd made the right life choices becoming a builder.

It was early days in the game when I knew Alan, but I knew my way around this environment. His was a part in a team of labourers whose job had been to gut out the interior of a fairly large executive home – one might call it a mansion! I remember Ted and I remember Dave and I remember John, Paul, Jim. I remember them chatting at tea breaks. Tea breaks were the main joy of labourers' life. At that time I didn't know about labourers: I knew what a plasterer did and I knew about electricians, and plumbers and carpenters. It wasn't until I asked my father "What does Ted actually do?" and he answered "He's a labourer" that I knew what a labourer was. Then I realised that *I* was a labourer.

Actually, at that time, my dad was a plasterer. His mate was Terry Golding. They were bloody good plasterers, and my job was to mix the plaster and serve it. There was this whole thing about what rooms were ready for us. We'd had a contract for the whole house but because it was in such disrepair – rooms without ceilings or floors, electrics not yet fitted, etc – we sometimes had to take on labouring jobs. It would otherwise have been a 'good earner'.

I gained my respect as a good worker on the day we screeded the main room. It was a huge job. Dad pepped me beforehand. "Because of the size of the room, we've got to get it done all at once. So it's going to be hard work: Terry will mix the gear, you'll barrow it in, and..."

I looked at dad anxiously for the ultimate result to doing all this hard work: would it be glory? Or money? Or would there be another hidden reason which he knew of?

"... and we'll get it done," he concluded with a nod.

We started early. Terry mixed the gear at the entrance of the long driveway where the sand and cement was dropped. I barrowed it down the drive, over precariously placed planks, and into the room. Dad collected the gear and levelled it down. It took us all day and we all worked really hard. It was the sort of job that seemed as though it would never end, and I was a heavy set young man – a fat lad really! So when we were done everybody congratulated us on working so hard. I was particularly commended on grafting very well, and really that's reward in itself. There's a rule or hidden nuance of being a builder, which is whether you're a grafter or not. I was gradually learning to be a grafter.

Samuel was the site foreman there at that time, but he wasn't doing a very good job. Some people didn't like him for whatever reasons, but I did. He said things that rung classic to me. When Jackson (a labourer) piped up with his ideas about what he thought should be done on a particular job, Samuel looked at him and said, comically, "Go on, fuck off!" That made me laugh. When the main hall was finally plastered and the industrial heaters were firing up to dry the plaster so that the painters could move in, he said, rubbing his hands together, "Go on, give it some!" That made me laugh. That latter phrase actually became a catchphrase I would use to motivate my band members before gigs.

This was a summer job. We'd previously done work in town on what was to be a stripper's club. My friend and bassist in the band, Alan, did a day's work with me on that. But also my best friend growing up, Steve, would begin his career in construction at this job in town. And also, Mark would join me at the summer job in Hampstead; we'd both left school.

Before you plaster a wall you have to make sure it's plasterboarded (or rendered) and the gaps in the plasterboard are scrimmed. Scrim is a sort of sticky tape made of grids of string. Plasterboarding was a good job; you got to put on your builder's belt that had a pocket of nails, a tape measure, a hammer and a Stanley blade. You measure up the area to cover, then mark the measurements on your plasterboard, then cut the board and hammer it in to place. It wasn't too messy a job and it made you feel good. It was my first foray into "skilled" labouring, that is, anything that wasn't carting bags of plaster up three levels on ladders, or mixing plaster, or cleaning up. It made you feel useful.

It was good to have Mark on site. He enjoyed to plasterboard too, although one day my dad, Fred, and me had to go off to pick up supplies and left Mark with Terry to cover the top floor woodwork in board. We got back; I asked Mark how it was and he said, "It was alright but that Terry's a fucking slave driver!" You'd find the odd newspaper around during teatime, and the one Mark liked was The Sport. He'd joke about the letter entries where readers would send in their saucy exploits. He laughed at the description, by a female reader, of a man's flaccid penis as a "sleepy, fat worm"!

It was a sunny job, it being summer – the best time to work in construction.

Samuel came up to our level, talking about Luke the plumber. That was the first I'd heard of Luke. Luke had been gossiping with Akhil about Samuel, and had bad mouthed him saying he didn't have a clue what he was doing. Akhil was the millionaire businessman whose house we were working on, and he knew Luke from the Old Finchlean's, which is a football club in North London. Samuel said, "I'll be honest, I don't like the bloke."

We were going up and down, as plasterers, to all different levels. That plan was to work our way down but, as I say, the rooms were not ready. In the conservatory, where we had to plaster the high ceiling, we were sitting down for tea. Akhil and his architects came in, but also Melissa, Akhil's wife. "You're always having tea!" she said. It was true, we always were!

"You only come in when we're having tea!" said Fred. Melissa was pregnant with James, her third child. After that we decided to make the effort to look busy when the customers were in the area.

Bernie was one of the electricians. He had this massive dog. I mean massive. Bernie used to smoke weed all day on site. He said he was Jamaican but he didn't look Jamaican. He'd stand by a point, smoking his spliff and wiring it up very slowly, and I'd be sweeping around the room, and he'd talk and talk about the soca scene in Kingston, and how the weed he's smoking is nothing compared to what you can get in Jamaica. He'd talk and talk.

Bernie's mate was Neil. Actually Bernie worked for Neil, who would go from room to room to organise the materials and electrical parts, and to dole out the labour to be done. He was a real good looking guy and had a great personality. You always wanted to talk to Neil and hear about his nights at clubs on ecstasy with fit models who wanted to have sex with him. You'd hear him say, eyes twinkling at the memory, "When *I'm* at the club, it's *me* up there on the stage having it; it's *me*!" And you'd know what he meant. Neil would have a puff, too. It turned out, he said, that the entire job was wired up stoned.

Luke was a plumber and so was Lee. Luke was this huge bloke with a giant grin that highlighted his massive jaw. Lee was a shorter bloke with a beer belly and he would always smoke Embassy king-sizes, and he'd hold it the right way too – like a dart. When I was carrying a bucket of rubble up a stairwell once, he tickled my bollocks for a laugh, and I told him to fuck off, and Jeff the painter saw it and said, "Oh, he didn't like that!" and Lee the plumber laughed.

At Christmastime Terry and dad went off to Samoa

on holiday, and I was given a labouring job in his absence. Terry and dad actually had gone there to build a house on some of dad's land. When they left they were replaced by two other plasterers, Charlie and Jack, for whom I had to work for the duration. Charlie was a young man back then. He was into kickboxing. Tall, thin and ginger – old Chuckie boy. Not a bad plasterer either. Jack was the father of one of the chaps who went to the same school as I did. He was a stocky, tough bloke and cocky too. In fact, it wasn't very good, my time working with these two.

Before he went, dad told me to just do whatever it was Jack needed, but no more; nothing unnecessary. We needed to plaster the stairwell to the basement, and I absolutely slogged my arse off for him one day, and he wasn't pulling his weight, Jack. In the end we had an argument – well, I had proper go at him. I didn't mean to; I was just so knackered.

There was this other bloke. He was a friend of Chuck's – I can't remember his name – bit of an arsehole. He liked George Michael. We had some banter, joked around. He seemed to like to rib me, and I saw it as an opportunity to show off my wit. But really he didn't like me and I knew it. He bullied me, really, a bit. When I was washing a bucket in a huge vat of water by the garage he chucked a tennis ball at my head. It really hurt; I can feel it now. And I told Terry, in a pub conversation after work one Friday when he was back in town, that he chucked a brick at my head. I mean, he didn't

– it was a tennis ball... I'd just said 'brick' so that I didn't sound like a wimp. I mean, it might as well have been a brick. But Terry was concerned and told my old man – that... whatsisname... threw a brick at my head. Dad confronted Chuck, but Chuck knew it was bullshit. It wasn't a brick; it was a tennis ball. But it felt like a brick. That Christmas we'd run out of work. I'd be scraping mud out of grooves in manhole covers it got as dire. So in the end they let me go. Samuel said, "Might as well call it a day, mate. If we hear of anything though..." But I was pleased.

Then eventually, when dad was back home, Akhil sacked Samuel and dad took on his work.

Dad was keen to do a good job. He certainly got things organised. He'd got bricklayers in whose job it was to lay the paviers on the path around the fair sized garden there. I don't remember their names, the two of them, but they just got on with it. I laboured for them quite a bit.

The whole thing started getting very stressful for old Fred. In fact, he changed a bit then. I'd never seen him so stressed. I suppose he wasn't the most popular man on site then. The bricklayer said, "Your old man walks round like a bear chewing a wasp!" The work got done eventually though, despite animosity from workers. And he'd have a puff! (Usually after work). He was still my old man.

It was the best time when the day would end. I'd finally get to sit in the van – this little Nissan thing –

and I'd roll up a spliff for me and I'd roll up a spliff for Fred. Usually they'd be these little roll ups with Golden Virginia and five seconds burn worth of hash two times. That's where my band name derived – Two Five Burn. And we'd sit there in the van and drive home, smoking our spliffs, listening to drive time on Radio One. The drive being forty five minutes we'd usually have two or three spliffs.

Once, Fred was ready to leave and he sent me to sit in the van, and I skinned up a massive weed spliff. It was skunk, actually. I started smoking it and was waiting for Fred, who always took ages adding the finishing touches to the day's work, and it was taking him forever – I suppose there was a lot to do that day. Anyway, he'd been an hour or so, and I was stoned off my face, then he comes up to the van, and I think 'Finally!' But then he says, "Dan, I've got a bit more to do. You might as well come back in and do some more – make yourself busy. So as I can put you down for the time." I didn't really want to do it, me being stoned as I was, but I didn't complain and I went back in.

It was one of them wintery January evenings, dark and cold, but warm with the business of workers working overtime in the light of the house. The stairs were being fitted, or the tilers were tiling, or both, and I walked round with a dustpan and brush and a plastic bag and started brushing the stairs. Virgin Radio was playing some Natalie Imbruglia or some such like pop song, and as I swept the little dust away I became self conscious of the fellow working on the stairs.

'Does he know I'm stoned?' I wondered. The guy was looking at me funny, I don't know why. Maybe it was because I was not doing a great job, or maybe because the work in hand was not entirely necessary, or maybe because I was giggling to myself for some unknown reason. I think he clocked me giggling, which added to my hilarity, and then I thought 'I've got to get out of here... I'm gonna piss myself laughing in a minute...' So I got up and quickly walked outside with a big shy grin on my face, chest huffing, went round the corner of the house, leant against the wall in the darkness, and pissed myself laughing.

In the end old Fred did do a good job on the house and soon he began to send Mark and I to another job a bit further down the road, for which Akhil got my dad in as site foreman. Our job as labourers was to strip the wallpaper in all the rooms, which we did stoned on hash, being that the house was empty and it was just us and our steamers and scrapers.

It took some while, perhaps a few weeks, but then Fred found a team to come in and tear down the ceilings; we were totally gutting the place. The team was me, Mark, Steve, Les Cooker, Terry Golding and Terry Shires (the two Terrys), and Peter. It was the dirtiest, filthiest job I've ever done: the amount of dust that comes out from inside the ceilings is unbelievable. We had masks and had to wet the rooms down continually. We had to carry the industrial strength bags of plaster and dust and 'lathes' (the strips of wood they used to nail to the joists so you could plaster the ceilings in the nineteen thirties or whatever) down three flights of stairs. After we'd done the first few rooms we had established a method, a routine, and we were flying.

Number 92 was remembered as a good job. Dad got in a great team – pretty much all the workers from the last site, except with different bricklayers and carpenters. This time Danny was the main brickie working on site. He was in his mid-fifties at that time. I had to knock up the gear for him. He used to sit in his chair at teatimes and let rip these horrible farts and say, "Cor! That was a ripper!" He used to get me tobacco from France, and I'd make his tea. People would wind the poor fellow up sometimes, chucking nails into his sand and cement: "Fucking shit gear!" he'd complain, and you'd see Lee the plumber giggling from a window above. Someone once nailed his boots to the ceiling. Danny was alright. He was ginger. He's dead now. Cancer.

And when that job was done we started on Akhil's next property on a private road nearby. Here we were the same team with added members: Barry and Dave the carpenters, and Bruce Turnby who drove a huge lorry, and Kevin Benjamin the plasterer and his mate Billy, plus other painters and decorators. The 'Courtney Avenue' job started off really well. We labourers had carpets to tear up and floorboards to rip out, and most of us were stoned the entire time. That was in the times when health and safety wasn't such a big issue.

The problem was not management. But Akhil and his architects couldn't come up with a decent plan for the house. Everything kept changing. A wall taken down one day had to be rebuilt the next day. A wall built one day had to be taken down the next. And everyone on site was on a day rate; there was no contract. Akhil was forking out the money and pretty soon a lot of the workers picked up on the fact that weren't making any appreciable progress. So, effectively, they started to take proceedings less seriously, that is, they wouldn't work as hard. In fact, they got very lackadaisical about proceedings. My dad, poor old Fred, was still stressed. Stress had become his personality, in a way, but he still worked, he still grafted, although spent a lot of time in the office, while the others skived off.

I mean, there was work being done, but in the end no effort was really being put in. Knowing that, say, a bin cupboard's foundation wouldn't be permanent meant that it would be done badly. But I was the boss's son so I had to work, and it seemed the other lads saw me as a bit of a brown nose. In any case, I was beginning to be ostracised. I definitely wasn't one of the most popular men on site, let's just say that. They all thought I was gay too, which couldn't be helped. I got a bit of stick for that, which I didn't enjoy because I was young man who had made some poor life choices and was at that time on drugs so much it made me very confused. I wasn't getting on well with the guys; I spent my days stoned, and on one occasion even went into work on a bad ecstasy pill. “You don’t look well, Dan,” said Shires. I wasn’t.

There was Marcus. He was a friend of Bernie’s – his mate as an electrician, actually – and was alright. He got me into these esoteric religious conspiracy books which came from a respective book shop in Holloway. He’d lent me two or three of them: they weren’t professionally published and were not written very well and I was sceptical of them at first. Marcus was a black guy who came to work telling everyone of the achievements of black men. The books were all about the New World Order, of which I’d not heard of up until then. But it was fascinating.

The books spoke about how everything is under control, from the Federal Exchange, to movies, to the language we use – for example, the word ‘understand’ was designed in such a way as to undermine truth in some way, and should really be ‘overstand’ instead. “Do you overstand?” the book kept saying. The point that was being outlined was, in effect, that the government had plans to bring about a New World Order, and as such was to be implemented by the introduction of identity cards, and not only those but, in effect, identity ‘transponders’ – microchips – to be injected into the right hand. This was a very bad thing – a terrible thing – because they contain the equivalent of barcodes... Every product on the planet has a barcode, and the thing about these is that each one – each and every one – has three sets of two lines longer than the other lines, which can be read as three times two equals six, with three sets... six-six-six, the mark of the beast!! Now, in Revelations, if you read it, it says, "He shall not buy or sell, he who has the mark of the beast in his right hand or on his forehead." So this was intended as an indication of the prophecy of the New World Order.

Further to this, there was more evidence! The pentagram, the five sided diagram, was the shape of the beast – thus the Pentagon in America! The books continued their symbolic theme. The eye of Horus, the triangle with the all-seeing eye inside of it, is on every American dollar bill. And furthermore the symbol was placed in surreptitious places in Hollywood films: in Indiana Jones, E.T. and suchlike, the symbol appears throughout. It was conspiracy! The perpetrators? The illuminati: a group of Satan worshipers who controlled all the money and government.

Then, as a supplement to the books, Marcus loaned me an underground video containing a documentary about the slyer dealings of the government, particularly the Federal Reserve. It was a history of money and how private banks control the economy. It was fascinating. What it said was that money only has value in accordance with what humans think it is worth. So, for example, in Jesus' time there were problems with money and so Christ went to the temple and struck out the money changers. That was all about coins of the day not having the ruler's head printed on it. Julius Caesar had made money plentiful, but soon came the dark ages. King Henry VIII devised a system of money made from branches, called 'tally sticks', in which value was indicated by notches carved down the length, and the branches were split and one half was given as receipt for the other half, and so on . The problem was usury, a system of banking that was made illegal, but is still used today, and which we call Fractional Reserve Banking. The gold smiths used paper money as a receipt for gold which was kept in banks. Soon they realised only a fraction of the people would take out their gold at any one time. This meant that banks were able to loan out ten times more money than they actually had and charge interest. To charge, say, eight percent interest on a loan of a hundred pounds means they would get back eighty percent interest. The bankers had a way of creating money out of nothing! Marcus' video described this conspiracy of the money changers to take control of the world economy.

It fascinated me greatly.

These new ideas about underground plans for the future of the world coincided nicely with other ideas I had come to believe, that were given to me in a self help book on the recommendation of Judy. It was called The Road Less Travelled by Dr M. Scott Peck. It was as important as the conspiracy books in every way! It's a famous book by a psychiatrist who develops a theory of love, good and evil, and the future of humanity. Love, he said, is the will to exert oneself to help people come to better spiritual health; evil is laziness and good is love;

the future of humanity is the dawning of the physical embodiment of God, that is, we're all going to become God! It sounds farfetched, but the way he put it – it was really exciting. That book was the first I'd heard of the theory of the collective unconscious. I remember the day after I finished reading it gazing at a tree almost seeing God saying hello.

Being in construction at that time, feeling as if I was an outsider, really wanting to have gone to university, reading these books was the closest thing I had to an education. I was still on drugs though, and although I had some good times and bad times, I had got lost in a world that was paranoid, and tense, and in which nobody knew what they were doing or why they were doing it.

Then Nine Eleven happened.

Hospital

The day after I had my arse handed to me by old sledgehammer feet in Mill Hill Broadway I woke up from a wet dream about sucking the loveliest pair of boobs I'd ever seen, in a strange room in a strange place that I still was not fully aware was a psychiatric hospital. I remembered the previous night with a shudder.

Having been evaluated by a health care worker, while inside the cell, two psychiatrists had been summoned that I might be investigated professionally. They looked at one another and the health worker as if to say "What's the problem?" when the cell door was opened, and they first saw me. "Take a closer look..." the health care worker seemed to say, as he motioned the psychiatrists in with a nod. They introduced themselves and told me they'd like to ask a few questions. The first was a tall man with shiny brown hair, and wore a suit and gave me a look that was full of official curiosity that turned to offended defensiveness after a short while. "How are you?" he asked.

"Fine," I answered.

“Do you know how long you’ve been in here?” he asked.

“About six hours,” I shrugged. The three men smiled at the accuracy of my estimate.

“What happened today?” asked the second doctor. He was a blonde man, slightly chubbier than the first, with glasses, and, at about forty years, the same age as the first. I explained the event, to their simultaneous concern. For some reason I felt then their enquiry deepen in intensity.

“Do you have paranoid thoughts?” went the first. I began to explore the spider web of my mind for a sufficient answer to this question, it being a challenge such that I might have the opportunity, to digress and therefore impress these men of higher learning, which does not always arise. Yet still being aware that I knew the right answer, it was a temptation too easy to submit to, and I began a short discourse into the types of thoughts anybody might have, which necessarily include paranoid ones. The two doctors, clearly impressed by my eloquence of speech, were now keen to further this investigation.

“Do you hear voices?” asked the first. Now, I knew that there was also a right answer to this question, curiously enough, one that I had been asking myself for a while in the previous months. I began again a short talk on the subject of mental volume, saying that, in effect, my thoughts themselves are loud, that is, I can hear them, so, in effect, to say that I do not hear a voice in my head, such as my thoughts are a voice and I can hear it, would be a lie.

I received a look that I did not recognise and can now only describe as the intellectual man's version of empty headed blankness. I felt then a kind of belligerence from both doctors, the blonde of which asked me a question that to this day I cannot remember what it was, but which I do remember having the need to take cue from a squashed up piece of dry tissue, that was stuck to the cell wall, thrown by previous inmate, that looked like a clown, for inspiration.

"...'Clouds'?" asked the blonde doctor.

"No, '*clowns*'," I corrected, in conclusion to his query, with a smile, and to his diligent satisfaction. They went out. I must have been in there for a good four more hours before I finally heard steps coming to the cell door, which was then unlocked. Prior to this – immediately, in fact – the hours of incarceration had culminated in a vision of the imagination of which I had not experienced the likes for some months. It caused me to see the necessity of such imprisonment, and I even felt a touch disappointed that I was to leave now, when after hours to myself I'd finally begun to think, and it was an image of myself as the 'loose cannon' that others must see me. It was vivid, and I was not ready to leave.

I remember, even before this, being asked if I wanted to go to hospital, and, thinking it to be the better option than staying inside the cell, and thinking it to be some lovely furnished room in which a wise old therapist would sit by my bed to talk of my thoughts and emotions. I said I would.

My jaw was aching; it was broken. At the desk where you collect your belongings I complained to the officer that I wished to press charges against old sledgehammer feet. "In two weeks," he'd said, to my dismay. With exasperation, I climbed in the police wagon.

The wagon door was opened, and I was motioned out at a place I did not know, where three people stood in a lobby with windows for doors. It was late at night and it was dark. The people, two women and a man, did not seem threatening. Yet I felt, as I stood before this building, that my urge to run would have been not only accepted by the officers there, but also encouraged. I would have run, but firstly I didn't know where I was, and secondly my ankle was sprained from jumping off a seven foot tall fence in Finchley last week. It was with happy resignation that I ignored the tacit expectations of the police, which I would later understand, and let the unthreatening people, who were nurses, escort me through doors ten feet from the lobby. "What's your name?" someone asked.

"Daniel," I told them as I passed through two sets of doors. I was led into a warm building with red carpets and to a room that smelled of plastic, and was plastic, and two African men stood looming large at the door, and an Asian woman, all with identity cards pinned to their chest. And there was a little blue mattress on the floor, and a cotton sheet, and there was a foam chair there that I sat on, as an old Irish nurse and another African man buzzed in and out together as if they were twins, of an organisation, and had a high position, but I knew they hadn't. My mobile phone was relieved of me as I sat on the foam chair in the room where the cumbersome African men and Asian woman, and now a Spanish man, stood at the doorway, all staring at me the way five year olds stare at the television, and I was told to sign a form. I smelled plastic or rubber as I signed it; I did not know what it was, except that they just took my phone, so it might have been for that. The twins buzzed in, seemingly inseparable, and gave water, then buzzed out again, together, buzzing. There was a conversation between this gaggle of who-the-fuck-knew-what-they-were mixture of strange people at the door, who could have been muscle or could have been muppets, but they certainly weren't brains. Theirs was a sense of confused hostility, which partially dissipated, as I endeavoured to arrive at the questions I should be asking, through my attempts to be friendly. A noble laughter at my uncertain jokes bubbled from their lips, and the twins buzzed in again, in a way you could have mistaken for professional expertise, this time to offer me a pair of tiny blue pills.

"Take them, they help you sleep!" insisted the African man. I refused, not trusting the effect or, to be honest, the source.

"Take them, take them!" insisted the Irish lady. Did they not hear me the first time?

"No thank you, I don't want them," I argued.

"Go on! Take them, they help you sleep!" the pair insisted. It was at this point I noticed that their eyes were askew – each of the twins were cross-eyed and looked strangely at me. It was a look that only now I understand to be the look of a demented idiot (not wanting to be unfair). I looked at the gaggle of strangers at the door, of which there seemed no discernible pattern as to describe them; no obvious regularity in their collective character, and then I saw that they each possessed the same demented appearance. To be honest, I was a little afraid!

"No thanks, I'm tired enough," I explained.

"Take them, take them!"

I nearly got angry at the two. Instead I accepted the pills and put them in my mouth and, without swallowing, hid them under my tongue.

The twins buzzed off, somehow placated in their work. The gaggle dispersed, I lay on the mattress, the light went out and I fell asleep. But not before spitting out the pills.

The time was about eight in the morning when I nervously left this plastic room and walked with curiosity into the empty corridor with the red carpet. A framed print of some landscape scene was hung by screws to the wall above a soft chair on my right, next to a door. On my left there was another chair, above which hung a pay telephone. The corridor opened out onto a junction where three other corridors went off in crossroad directions, and a room with windows was a corner of this junction, and it said 'Day room'. There was a man standing just by the door like a guard and had an identity card hanging from his neck. He said good morning, and I asked his name, and he asked mine.

"Raymond," he'd said without urgency. I still hadn't crystallised the questions that were floating in the back of my mind. I did not know where I was, what I was there for, or what was going to happen. There was a chair and I sat in it.

Then, as I took in my surroundings, noticing a room before me with some activity going on inside and a sign saying 'Office', the scene was ornamented with the appearance of quite the strangest and perplexing looking lady I had ever seen. Thin and of average height, wearing loosely fitting pyjama bottoms with sandals and slightly dirty blouse, I noticed her arms and their scars of cuts in those, that had healed, and she had brown unwashed and unkempt hair and had glasses behind which were set the most bulging eyes I had ever seen. "Are you new?" she enquired with plain trust, and she asked me my name, and I told her, and asked hers, and hers was Annie. "Do you smoke?" she asked without eye contact. I thought then that her implication was to see if I had any that she could acquire. In fact I hadn't smoked for two days, and though was toying with the idea of stopping, I decided after the events of yesterday that now was not the ideal time to do so, and after a moment's thought I said I did, but had none.

"I'll find you a cigarette," Annie asserted with the same plain trust. "Abdul! Have you got a cigarette?"

To my right was a room with a sign that said 'Smoking room', and Abdul was in it. The room smelled of damp fag ends, there were purple chairs lining two walls, there were two coffee tables of the same design as the chairs, and a soft phase of sunlight beamed in from the high windows and left half the room in shade. Abdul passed Annie a cigarette, Annie passed it to me, and I went in and sat opposite Abdul. He was a Somalian in his early twenties, had a plain blue t-shirt and jeans, and he was barefoot. He was engaged in the act of smoking, which was his entire preoccupation. His bony fingers tapped at the cigarette as flakes of ash flew all over the table, including into the ashtray, as he stared with a sort of neurotic frustration or impatience at the area of flicked ash. I tried to spark a conversation, by telling him my name, but to no effect, and I became a touch uneasy, and swallowed in recognition of the growing peculiarity of the new environment. A nurse had lit my cigarette, and I took a pull out of it. Unconscious questions lay undeveloped in my mind still.

Gradually the morning drew on, and the reception area slowly blossomed with the faces of more decided oddities of humans, some of which I soon discovered were psychiatric nurses, the rest of whom were patients, all of whom shared a spookily strange serenity which I could not quite engage with.

In a room opposite the smoking room, with a sign

that read 'Dining room', a breakfast of tea, toast and cereal had been served with a procedure I knew was tinged with regularity despite it being my first. As I struggled painfully to chew my cornflakes my jaw clicked and stung. The windows here provided a view of a square patch of grass lawn that some gardeners were mowing, and I noticed its edges to be enclosed with a high fence that had barbed wire around the top. I was glad of a sip of tea. Knives and spoons were handed out according to a list that was ticked by a nurse sitting at the doorway, with a clipboard. Leftover food and trash was to be scraped into a basin, bowls and cups to be left on the trolley. I left the room, with questions burning to be crystallised, and wandered round the rooms and wondered what to do.

By midmorning the place had become fairly busy, a fact made more evident by the hurried business of two staff in particular, Ahmed and Meena. They were both Indian and both behaved with a professionalism, that could not be extended to the two staff of the previous night, yet that had a humour in it, and was cause of a certain relaxation of tension here. Meena, who would dash from the office to the other several rooms here, and back to the office, giving orders to staff and easing the concerns of patients on the way, was the head nurse. I tried to grab her attention, that I may corner her and see if an unsettled feeling in my mind could be fully borne out. But all she would say was, "Wait, you will see doctor Anni..." and rush off to another room. Still, I only felt the uncertainty akin to being in new surroundings, and no urgency or immediate worry as to my situation here. Still, I felt with some self-assurance that soon I would be informed, and back at home before dinner. I was confident of it.

Ahmed wore a badge identifying him as the ward manager, and walked with the same authority as did Meena, but with more office. As I stood in the reception area he asked me how I was, and without giving too much away, informed me of the occupational therapy group activity that would take place in the dining room at two pm. As Ahmed started to move on to his next task the very round figure of a person my age, who wore a skull cap, trotted up to my side and, with a raspy voice, asked, "Are you Jewish?"

"No," I replied, and with a subtle sincerity said, "but I'd like to be!"

He walked away, not so much with disappointment, but a regarded lack of positive impression, and I wondered at my mistake. Soon I began to gain confidence in my surroundings and started to try to converse with patients. From the reception I could look into the day room where I saw a most angry looking individual pacing in a small area, glaring menacingly at the floor, and seemingly engaged in a personal conflict that left him grimacing and shaking his head. Yet despite this aggressive appearance something told me he was not going to be a great problem, physically at least. He had the air of a sweet dog that was big but gentle, and I was surprised he had not yet made eye contact.

I found myself milling in the doorway of this room, and there was another Indian fellow, my age, sitting patiently in a soft chair with his head right back. He looked, to be frank, stunned. I walked up to him with a cocksure attitude, that had been slowly entering back into my head with the familiarity that time here forged upon me, and introduced myself.

"I'm Dan, what's your name?"

It was Ashley. He wore glasses and looked quite clever. "You look quite clever," I ventured, and challenged, "have you been to university?" I had been to college and knew about intellectual conversations. You have conversations about university, if you are intellectual. He had been, and got a first in computer science. Ashley was friendly, in the sense of being approachable, but was still a touch guarded. Yet he had the same strange air possessed by every patient I'd seen.

"Why are you here?" I smiled, investigating not only into his own story but also for clues about my own fate.

"I committed a crime," he sighed with resignation, and almost continued but didn't. He might have divulged the perpetration, but I think, taken aback by the very nature of his admittance being criminal, and this being a psychiatric hospital, I smiled self-satisfactorily and walked away. He must have thought me odd for doing so, for he looked at me most confusedly, as I hopped off.

Still, I was not yet clear about the reasons why I

was here, and what was going to happen. So I decided to seek some sensible inspiration from a certain means of communication in the form of a letter, and began writing one to my grandfather in New Zealand. I remember that the words seemed full and large, as I huddled down at a ledge beneath a television in the day room, and I described what I could about the events that led me in this place. But I also remember that only a short paragraph was finished before I was summoned to the dining room to engage in an activity with several other patients, and an attractive young woman who was leading this odd group, at a game of trivial pursuit.

On my left was sat a huge Jewish man whose name was Gershon, and he had a beard and suit on with the type of hat that is worn by orthodox Jews, and was very friendly, yet his character was that of an overgrown toddler, and he laughed and joked. Next to him was sat an Irishman, pale like a tired out car salesman in forlorn looking old sports clothes. Abdul was in there and he would sit for one minute, then walk around, leave, and come back in. A young man not eighteen, named Steven, would gaze with distracted thought at his hands, not looking around. He seemed studious too, as though fresh from A-levels.

And among all of these, at the far end of the table, I had made meaningful eye contact with an older man. He wore glasses, had grey hair and features, a grey shirt and blue cardigan, was thin as though malnourished, and replied embarrassedly (yet with a hint of curiosity and hope) with a look, at the promise which was contained in my surreptitious communication. We were flirting! And the promise was culminated in the threads of wisdom and knowledge that I had, was seeking to learn how to impart, and I also had hope then, and began to see a new role I could play in this place.

The game ended, the group dispersed, and I went back into the smoking room, to sit. I had sparked my Marlborough, obtained from which source I now fail to recall, but contentedly smoked with a mild frustration, not yet borne, at the unasked questions in the back of my mind.

Then the raspy voiced, round Jew with the skull cap walked in (I was alone) and plonked himself in the chair opposite me, his cigarette already sparked, and quite deliberately and intensely began to stare me in the face. He took a drag.

"Alright?" I asked, mild frustration now brought up a level to middling. He said nothing, took another puff, and continued his purposeful stare. It was one that did not ring friendly in the slightest, and after a few seconds I resolved to rectify the situation, it being that his stare contained a sense of passive-aggression, as though he questioned my ability to do anything about it. We were away from any company, and I took my opportunity. "What the fuck are you looking at?" was my inquiry.

His expression went from a look of "Fuck you" to a look of "I'm in trouble now!" and his face slowly turned from a threatening grimace to a helpless grin, but he continued his stare. I took offence and my face became filled with anger. "What's your fucking problem, ya dickhead?!" I asserted. "Fucking keep looking at me like that and I'll fucking knock you out, ya cunt!" I finished my cigarette, stubbed it out, and left the room. He was still grinning.

The next few hours went by without a great deal of activity. The back door had been opened at a convenient stage, and patients allowed out into the garden. There was a basketball court and I played a couple of shots.

North Finchley

I was in the smoking room among a group of others, and it was about seven o'clock, when Meena approached me with news that my mother was here and she was waiting in the interview room. 'Finally,' I thought as the nurse took me through, 'I'm going to get out of here.' I entered the room and saw my mother waiting, with an angry look on her face. Her handbag was on her lap. I sat down. Mum really was not best pleased at all. "You've been a stupid boy again, haven't you," she said.

Mum thought me unwell for a long time. When I lived in Finchley, after I had proved to be too difficult to live with, and dad had found me a room there, mum was so worried that she took me to a doctor. I'd met my parents at home, and we all walked down to the surgery on Hartley Avenue. We sat quietly in the waiting room; I would try to make polite conversation with mum. She would be distracted, full of concern, unable to understand the complexity of my words, and looked about as though the room was a dark forest, and I was unable to see the problem. Dad would pick up a magazine and flick through it.

The doctor called us in, me and mum, and dad waited outside. The GP was our family's, Dr Waites.

"What seems to be the problem?" began Dr Waites.

"There's something wrong with Daniel," mum explained. She felt I was alien to her, that I would not be able to talk sense, that I had been writing incomprehensible things, that I was not myself. Dr Waites urged me to talk. I looked about the office and noticed the sunlight beaming in the room, and noticed a bookshelf, the computer and a printer. I began to talk with fevered animation, and gesticulated wildly without the foggiest idea what I was talking about, as Dr Waites calmly tried to make sense of my words. As the doctor watched and listened, I had the distinct need to impress her, her being a woman of higher learning, and tried to be as intelligent as I could be. I think my discourse was full of every idea I'd had. I'd go on about the genius of religion or free will or melon, and joke about the plans of the new world order, or how foliage was able to communicate, or how music was time. When I was satisfied that I had convinced Dr Waites of my sanity, intelligence and brilliant sense of humour I became quiet and looked over to mum.

She was in a state of total and utter terror. Her shoulders were hunched up, her eyes near to tears, and viewed me with a look of complete unrecognisability, that I became more concerned about her and thought perhaps the doctor should see *her* rather than *me*. I wanted to ask if she was alright, but this inquiry would never find its way to fruition. I think the doctor mentioned that she would add a note to her computer and communicate with the services. But eventually we left, and I walked to town to get a pizza.

It was a hot day in August, I noticed, as I rode the 221 back to Finchley with a full stomach after a visit to Pizza Express. It was the sort of day that you might benefit from a dip in the pool. Finchley has a pool, so when I'd returned to my room I thought I'd go along. In fact I fell asleep for several hours, and dreamed about the last two weeks.

Julian was the owner here, at this flat above a kebab shop from the Tally Ho pub. He seemed like a reasonable man. A bald ginger giant with glasses and a job in government, he shook my hand with anticipation when first he accepted me as a tenant. I thought I might like to have a pint with him, and there was no shortage of pubs around here, and would ask if he would like that. He never did.

But I would make it a general preoccupation to visit the local bars and make the most of being outside. However, not amassing a huge amount of money, I would have to drink pints of water, and also I would steal.

My big realisation, that actually everything should be free; that people only pay for things through fear and conditioning, that is, we fail to question the social protocol of standing in a queue, or the laws of theft, well, it dawned on me as I realised I was able to walk into a supermarket, collect a basket of items, walk out without paying for it, all totally under the radar of everyday shoppers. I'd even figured out that it was possible to fill up a shopping bag with groceries at the counter, in full view of the attendant, provided you had the confidence to do such a thing. My observation was that people rarely checked about themselves, and I took advantage of this and was able to feed myself for free. That's how I saw it.

The same realisation contributed to the way I would conduct myself on the streets and in bars. I felt like I was above everyone, and would approach anybody and talk to them. "You there," I said to two African ladies walking slowly in the heat. "Pick up your feet woman!" It cheered them up immensely. "Alright chaps!" I greeted, in address of a Mediterranean grocery store, as the staff inside grinned happily at my confidence. "What a lovely shop you have here! So apt too, that it's Spanish! Are you from Spain? You brought the sun with you! Or is that a coincidence? Any free juice?"

I walked to Argos to judge the veracity of my realisation. I was willing to test it upon the establishment with the relief of some electrical goods. A lovely young blonde lady was waiting on a chair. "Isn't it fascinating, the similarity of shopping for products and looking for lovers?!" I proposed. She laughed nervously with eyes of helpless submission. "We may as well get married now, love!" But I got distracted and left. I had not stolen any electrical goods.

Soon I felt the kind of alienation from society that comes with a beautiful mind, and as a result my conduct became more extreme. One Saturday I decided to walk the streets with my bible and go around reading random passages to strangers. I had gone into a bar, and without a great deal of belligerence, found a group of people and began my sermon. The passage was from Genesis; the point I was making was that the word is good and God is good. I would read the excerpt and, to their amusement, had the entire pub's attention. A group of lads were playing pool, and I went among them, and read from the bible out loud, yet there was a little belligerence if I'm being honest. Said belligerence became saturated in the goodness of God's word, yet I left before I got a kicking.

Julian had locked me out, it seemed, as I tried my key in the keyhole. The key fit the lock but I was fully aware that, whether by design or accident, Julian had double locked the door. It was infuriating. I banged and shouted. There was no reply, yet I knew my landlord was home. I had a mobile phone but no credit. Besides, I didn't know the telephone number of the apartment. I gave up and went across to the pub. I had no money on my person. "Er, hello," I said to the bar lady at the Tally Ho. "This might sound funny to you but the thing is that I've just moved in across the road and my landlord's locked me out but my money is in my room there, so I was wondering, love, would it be a huge imposition if I could have a pint and I would pay you back later, I promise!"

The bar lady explained to me how this wouldn't be possible, sorry, so I said, "Ah, okay, then can I have a pint of water?" Several patrons had been casually listening in and were visibly impressed and relieved at my resolve.

Later on, I decided I hadn't banged the door hard enough, and I went back to the flat to have another try. This time it worked; Julian was here.

"What's the matter, doesn't the key work?" he smiled.

"You double locked the door," I accused.

"I didn't!"

But I knew he did. A few days later, I resolved to exact revenge by double locking the door on *him*. He was really angry when he couldn't open the door to his own home. I basically got evicted for doing this.

I woke up after the dream still full from my pizza. It was stiflingly hot. The open window was not letting in any draft. It was dark, about two in the morning. A nice dip in a cold pool would be exactly the right sort of thing. Finchley had a pool, and it was just down the road, and I put on my swimming shorts and walked to the Lido. The walk took slightly longer than I thought, so I was relieved when I finally got there. I knew that there was an outdoor pool and had to think how I would navigate over the seven foot tall fence.

Now on either side of the fence there were large containers each seven foot tall and easy to climb. But the gap between was too wide to jump across. Contemplating the fall that would come from simply jumping from the box to the ground, and thinking I'd not get hurt that badly, I decided to jump. I cleared the fence, from box to ground, and went into a military roll, but the fall was harder than imagined and I'd hurt my ankle. However, it wasn't too bad, and I went for a dip, which required me to yank back the pool cover, and it being an unbelievably hot night, I lay in the cool water for an hour.

A night worker pushed a trolley through the area, and I considered this a bonus, since I daren't jump from the inside container to get out again, and worse comes to worst, I might need his help. He hadn't seen me. My ankle was becoming even more painful. When my swim was done I left the pool and went back to the fence to find my way out. There being two huge containers placed like this, I thought, 'I wouldn't be surprised if someone had left a long plank to join them.' It was fortunate that my instinct was correct; there was a long plank. I used it to crawl between the high containers, and was thankfully able to escape without further injury. But the walk home took even longer than I imagined, my ankle was badly sprained, I limped pitifully, and it took forever.

At six o'clock that morning I called my mother saying that I felt sick from pain. She explained with exasperation that this was adrenaline and added that she had spoken to Julian, that I was being evicted, and she would be there to pick me up shortly.

So here I was, back at home. Suffering from my sprained ankle made it difficult to keep busy in any physical way, yet I found myself still needing to seek refuge in bars, and one day had been at one nearby, which was a sports bar. I was sat on a stool with a forlorn frustration exuding from my countenance, perhaps put there by the unfortunate events of the previous week, capped by further alienation, and feelings of hostility, from members of the public. The patrons in this bar, playing pool and watching football, could sense my distress, could see I was not best pleased, and began to become agitated at my unperturbed and passive-aggressive glares. Two or three I had known from school; one or two others were new faces, and I found humour in the agitation of the latter. It was a shorn headed and well built, stocky young man who felt the necessity to turn his face to mine and make the motion to accept a fight: "Come on then!" he seemed to say, but with subtlety, so that when I made not to notice, he was able to confusedly continue his shot. I knew I had to go, and I left.

I think I must have had about five or six pounds on me, and I thought I quite fancied seeing a film. The bus stop was right there, and I went to it to wait for the 113.

It can be a very lonely old world at the best of times. They say you can feel very lonely in the countryside, and while that may be true, you can live in the city and be surrounded by people and still feel lonelier than you know. The London underground is an extremely good example of such a phenomena, it being such that much of the time they are filled with silent strangers facing each other without a mere notion that there could be an opportunity for exchange. I think that is a failing of society, and that the reason we say nothing is because we don't know what to say. What we've not yet realised is that strangers are just friends we haven't met yet. I would often see society as something I could change – millions of people on tubes and buses all afraid to trust each other – and I would talk to people. I would talk to people at bus stops.

I was stood at the bus stop there at Fiveways, and I reflected on these thoughts, and there was a young man sitting with his golf clubs. I felt, rightly or wrongly, this was a good opportunity for a chat. So I said, "Nice set of clubs mate. You off to Mill Hill?" At this the young man turned abruptly and scowled at me.

"Whassat?!" he said rudely, and tinge of anger crept up my spine.

I'd had good intentions in approaching this person, I'm sure. But as the young man turned away, and I reflected on such rejection, anger overflowed and surged up into my head, and I burst out into his face, my finger pointing, right into his face, "You little fucking shit! I was trying to be friendly, you fucking little prick! You're fucking lucky I don't lamp you now." And I hadn't punched him; I knew he was too young. But I picked up his golf clubs, pointed at his face one more time and said, "You've fucking lost these."

He nodded in understanding, and I walked off carrying the clubs. As I got to the corner of the road I heard the lad shouting for help outside the sports bar. "Help! Someone's just stolen my golf clubs!"

Some of the patrons of the bar came to his aid, and as I limped up the road, I was followed by lad who called to me from a distance. "Mate! Give 'im back 'is clubs!" he shouted in a friendly way. "Come on mate, don't be like that! Give 'im back 'is clubs!"

I shook my head, still fuming at the young man's rudeness.

"Come on! Don't be like that!"

Some other older men were walking behind the friendly lad, and I heard them say, "Let's get the van," and I knew I was in trouble. In my head I was assessing all the choices I had: - I couldn't run; shame, because I'd have run to the shrubs of the fields up the road – I couldn't take out the clubs and set about using them in any conflict. I'd have to dump the clubs and see how far I get. I did dump the clubs, into the front lawn of a nearby house, but I took out one for protection.

I limped as fast as possible, and now my plan was to try to make it to the alleyway on Longfield Avenue. I visualised the beating I would get if the men in the van caught up with me. The van was coming up the road and I was out of options.

Then, as though the entire debacle was engineered by God in my favour, a red Vauxhall Astra pulled out at the corner of Longfield Avenue, and I recognised it to be driven by my old bassist and friend Alan, who lived on that road. I praised the Heavenly Father and ran around the front of the car, opened the boot, said, "Alan, you've got to save me!" and jumped in. I closed the boot door just as the men in the van turned into the avenue, and I breathed in relief. To them it must have seemed like I had disappeared. Alan took me home by the long route, at my instruction. I gave him the taken club, which was a putter.

A few days later I was visited by the crisis team. It was mum's desire that I let them assess me; she had asked my permission. In fact, she had begged me to see them. And I'd said fine. It was Monday or a Tuesday at two or three o'clock when the team were invited inside. There was an Indian doctor and an Indian nurse, and a white woman with blonde hair who may or may not have been a social worker. They took a seat in the living room, and mum was to sit on her knees on the carpet, and I came in and sat on the sofa. I was greeted with familiar unperturbed looks of incomprehension. The team introduced themselves before the questions came. There was a blue suitcase in the room.

How is it fair that certain people are given the authority to ask particular directed questions, that we are obligated to answer, as if being tested on topics we've had no training in how to answer correctly, or any interest in giving a 'correct' answer, or even knowing that there *is* a correct answer? How is it fair that certain people are allowed to probe into the personal thoughts of individuals, which are none of anyone's business, and upon which the entire mental state of a person can be decided, and upon which said individual can be judged? It's an imposition! And it's an imposition that was to occur frequently through the following years of my life.

I did not like the Indian doctor. He was cold and humourless. I did not like the white social worker. She seemed lost and confused. I may or may not have liked the Indian nurse. She appeared dispassionate. The questioning from the Indian doctor would lack any genuine attempt at connecting with me, and I think I actually have cast the memory of his exact enquiry out. But when the social worker asked me how I feel when I go out, I saw this more as a cry for help on her part, being that I saw a helpless dread in her eyes. So I proceeded to talk about how, when I go out, it could be considered very scary because people can be mean and cruel, but that's just a facade, and when you get to know people, you find that they like to chat and that they're not so scary after all, that they're more scared of you than you are of them, and it's alright, and I like to go out and I recognise that there *is* the fear of hostility, but you have to take that sort of thing within your stride, and rise above it. In my eyes I was doing the lady a service, trying to ease her unconscious concerns about the ways of the outside world, in my own style. In any case, when I had done, the team requested five minutes to discuss their observations, and mum and I left the room.

Five minutes later we were called back in, and I sat in an armchair to hear their considerations. I anticipated a favourable result but was disappointed to hear they believed I had "disordered thoughts", and they were going to take me to hospital. "No," I argued. "You're not." I didn't want to go to any hospital and certainly couldn't see myself going happily along with such a plan.

"Yes, you are," was the response from the social worker with a look of smug authority, and with a slightly personal attitude, which clearly must have been borne from my perhaps improper exposing of her inner approach to social experience. In any case, in truth I panicked, and angrily (to say the least) stood up with a shot. "GET THE FUCK OUT OF MY HOUSE!!" I yelled with all the intimidation and aggression I could manage. "WHO THE FUCK DO YOU THINK YOU ARE?! COMING IN 'ERE, ORDERING ME ABOUT?"

The feeling of their shock, as it had quickly dawned upon them that I was not best happy at their presence, and their sunken way in which they all moved out of the house, caused me not a small amount of satisfaction. "GO ON, KEEP GOIN' YA PRICKS!!" I roared, while mum stood helplessly in the hallway, behind me. "WANKERS!" I shouted conclusively as they went to their vehicle.

The sun had been shining brightly up to this point, and I had got my way; yes, I had got out of another situation. And then, quite suddenly and heavily, it began to pour with rain.

Techno

It was obvious I wasn't very well. At least it was to me. The prolonged years of drug misuse had taken its toll, and even if the nights at clubs and raves had seen me shine, in the way you're meant to shine in these times, it's true that the come down left me to be something of a sad case. I was stripped of all hope, despairing at dead and gone dreams, and only had eyes for peak time at the parties – an image of pure ecstasy at the height of a drug rush, when you would look around and see all eyes on you, and you'd be in heaven, and so would everyone else – and I'd single mindedly seek that that experience, better than sex, and it was all I could think about. But even that scene was getting old. I clung to it. Many people did. As a result my mind and brain suffered, and as I huddled under sheets, hiding from reality, repetitious thoughts would run through my head. I knew I wasn't very well, but only wondered by what miracle nobody else had noticed.

I went along the same destructive pathway, getting progressively worse, gradually deteriorating, and becoming more and more alien to those around me. Sometimes I'd be invited off on a trip – Amsterdam, Magaluf, Bournemouth – but could never quite work out why I wouldn't have a very good time. In Amsterdam I'd spent much of the time confined to the hotel room, tripping on magic mushrooms, while the ones I'd gone with – Gary, Ben, Nilesh – appeared to be having a great time. I remember the Magaluf holiday with the boys; it should have gone so well, but I could not engage with it.

You're supposed to go to Magaluf so that you can have sex with loads of girls, but I was having great difficulty connecting with anyone. I couldn't have pulled a plug that holiday. In any case, I got frustrated, one evening getting lost on the island and finding myself at the edge of a fence outside a bar and barking at the patrons at it like a dog for ten minutes, all the while shaking the fence, and nobody took a blind bit of notice; nobody laughed, nobody shouted, nobody said, "look at that nutter!" I was totally out of touch.

You're not supposed to fight when you're in Spain because the Guardia Civille will take you straight to jail, and I knew that. But one evening, having politely asked a holiday maker for a spare cigarette, I was told to fuck off, and such an attitude caused my temper to boil over, and I smashed my glass on the floor and started shouting at the man. I told him to get the fuck up 'cause I was gonna knock him out; I was gonna fucking knock him out! I was unaware that the man was accompanied by several other large men who were visibly shocked by my conduct in this matter, yet who were also privy to the legacy of the Spanish police and consequently watched with concern, as my tirade ended in the fortunate circumstance that I was dragged out of the situation by two of my loyal friends, Gary and Andrew. It was a highly frustrating holiday. One night I had left a bar with familiar dissatisfaction, walked back to my hotel room and just burst into tears, crying, "What's fucking wrong with me?"

The Bournemouth trip wasn't a great deal better. Ben Kelson drove up, and Steve was there, and Ben's friend who I didn't know. We'd gone to a club, and Steve had instantly pulled and taken his prize back to the hotel room. Now, I was supposed to share that room with Steve, so I had to sleep in Ben and his mate's room. And Ben had a huge bag of pills and I took one or two, and lay down to get some rest. If you've ever tried sleeping on ecstasy you know you won't have much luck. But I tried, and I was tripping out, and Ben and his mate were trying to sleep, and I tripped out so hard that I blurted out some completely random sentence that I do not know what it meant, but it freaked Ben out, so he told me to go and sleep on the beach.

None of those holidays were any good, really. I was addicted to drugs still, and I couldn't see a way out, yet I knew something had to change. Then something did change.

When 9/11 happened, and in the time leading up

to it, I was consumed with turmoil. My inner thoughts were engaged by the question of my sexuality. I remember realising that in life, when it comes to sexual preferences, you're faced with a choice. I realised that you're not necessarily born one way or the other, but can make a decision for yourself about what it is you want. Needless to say, at this realisation, I chose to be straight, and this was my choice. But after 9/11, when everyone began talking about who did it – was it terrorists or an inside job? – it became easier to communicate.

Having read fairly widely into the esoteric side of things about the attacks, I had formed my own beliefs about why it happened and who did it. I collected and read newspapers every day about it. However, I found I was (without wanting to sound too isolated) solitary in my fascination. Despite all the excitement, and the renewed political fervour, I don't remember a great deal of genuine discussion as to the overwhelming possibilities. To be sure, there was heightened saturation in the media; greater and helpless faith in that, but what I hadn't seen was considered interest in the, admittedly conspiratorial, prior fears and concerns that led up to it. I imagine that, to many people, the attacks happened and that was it; it didn't mean anything to them. To them it marked no conscious shift in culture or society. Needless to say, what with my political ideas hitherto, it meant something to *me*.

And as I say, the tensions which I had felt very deeply had eased, and I was able to think things through, and do that with refreshed optimism and positivity. So one night as I settled in to watch television with a hash spliff in my bedroom, I mulled over my choice of sexual preference, and finding my thoughts to be had in the form of a clearly repetitive object, I realised something.

Sometime later – months later – after a period of genuine amazement, I was stood at the back of a London gay club at the bar.

Resplendent music such as Michael Jackson, and harsh neon strobe lighting filled the room, while different sorts of young men danced on the podium in the centre. I had gone alone, being that my friends were not the type of people to have joined me, and mine was a beer in a plastic cup. But it didn't bother me I was on my own, because every so often I would find myself in a conversation with some guy there. The guys standing next to me seemed driven to motion by a tall, dark haired man who was in clothes that reminded me of Jean-Paul Gaultier in blue. He struck up a conversation – asked me where I'm from, why I was alone. I think his name was Anton. He breathed over me with the breath of an alcoholic. "How did you know you were gay?" he asked. I told him: I was watching television in my bedroom one night, and it just occurred to me. I don't think he was able to fully understand my realisation, but we both agreed it was fine thing to be able to admit to yourself.

Anton, it turned out, was an asshole, which he freely accepted, and though we had a dance, I went home alone.

The day after my revelation, I was filled with a sense of freedom. With certainty of mind, my approach to any gender at all seemed to have been liberated.

The thing I'd understood was only that we deny ourselves because that's the way society conditions us: we think we're not allowed to be who we are. We could accept ourselves, and would, if we knew that the benefits of alternative decisions were equally as approachable as those which we keep within the sacrifices of our own hang ups. It's as good to choose uncertain paths, if not better, for a vast number of reasons.

I was to have an easy day, this day, for my agenda was to go to a Finchley dentist, instead of work. Buzzed in, I came into the waiting room and noticed that the receptionist was a beautiful young brunette. I thought now I could get up and ask her on a date. The dentist called me through.

He wore horn-rimmed glasses, a studious looking pale green cardigan over a shirt, grey trousers, and was ginger, and at about thirty five, looked like a type of Mister Garrison. Our tacit glance on introduction would reveal the surreptitious news of my outing, and he lay me down in the chair. The chair was low, and as he pumped it to raise it up I noticed his crotch was in line with my thigh; he was close. And then as the chair was raised, and my thigh rubbed his crotch, I visibly shuddered at the discomfort of the encounter. As he looked in my open mouth, somehow satisfied at my failed initiation into the ranks of being okay with inappropriate advances, I wondered at the notion of filing a report against him for the deed. But I knew that in fact it wasn't a problem.

After my appointment I followed the dentist back in the waiting room, and thought about how easy it would be to ask the beautiful brunette receptionist on a date. Mister Garrison flipped through some administrative notes, as I resigned myself to missed opportunity, and I noticed, to my left, a mother with her child was staring at my countenance with curious anticipation, and her being just out of view, I turned to her as if to say, "Yes, I know: I'm gay." And she was happily placated.

I had to wait for a bus going to work in Hampstead. The stop was over the road from the dental practice, and I sat alone. A minute or so had passed before I felt the same curious anticipation coming from my right. In my head I got the idea of a source that I would not usually have acknowledged, like one of those mean, straight men. But suddenly I was aware that I knew who I was and hence had nothing to hide and no reason not to face up to the oppression of such unsatisfied anticipation. And then, in my head, as I turned, I imagined a beautiful gay man who would see my freshly informed face and smile and meet me and become my great friend and lover. Yet it was only a seventeen year old young man walking along the road, who looked at me with such innocence that I inwardly scoffed, and thought, "So that's who I've been afraid of!"

So, much of the tension of previous times had been

concluded. On the Hampstead building site, although still early days for me, things started improving, socially. I chatted with cautious confidence with men whom I had had difficulty doing so before. I began to notice their qualities – of their minds, as much as anything. I began to hear different aspects of the language they would use, and their intentions of using them; the things they would say, and the things they would really mean.

Adam was new on this site, relatively, and Steve was there and he'd have a laugh with Adam. One day towards the end of the job, Steve wanted to hear Adam say particular things, it being that Adam was Middle Eastern and was new to speaking English. So Adam was down a foundation ditch, and Steve said, "Adam, say: 'I'm a raving homosexual!'" Andy laughed and in his Iranian accent said, "I'm a raving homosexual! I said it, so what!!"

"Are you a raving homosexual, Adam?" said Steve jocosely.

"Yeah, I'm a raving homosexual! So what? I said it!"

Adam was not homosexual, you understand. And I was there watching, and Steve turned to me, shovel in hand, and said, "Are you a raving homosexual, Daniel?"

I'd had a problem with it before. I'd vehemently deny it; I'd get pissed off with it; I'd get visibly upset about it. It was about a week or two after my revelation, and as Steve stood there on a heap of rubble, shovel in hand, waiting for a reply, I toyed with the idea of going,

"Naah!" which would have been fine.

Instead I looked at him, shrugged, and nodded unapologetically, "Yep!" To my left Terry Shires, a great friend of my father's, looked down embarrassedly as he pushed a wheelbarrow through the yard.

I'd outed myself.

****

But drugs were still in my life, and in addition I was still in a relationship with Judy – admittedly an uncertain one. She liked to hang out with me, and I her, but I didn't know if I was her boyfriend or not.

Sometime after my revelation Judy took me to a club. She was friends with a seasoned homosexual called Paul, and brought him along too. It was a house and techno club at London Bridge, to which I'd brought a stack of ten ecstasy pills wrapped inside a roll of rizla paper, and smuggled them in on the inside of my palm. They never clocked me on that.

We had gone in, the three of us, and bought our drinks, water or Redbull or Coke, whatever. Judy wore these fun and attractive black fluffy boots which went with her black fluffy mini-dress and tights and she had a black fluffy jacket and all manner of bright, neon adornments: necklaces, bracelets, hair things. She had an impatient air this night, borne of what frustration I did not know. At the beginning of the night, after we got our drinks, she'd gone missing, and I sat with Paul not really saying very much. He wasn't talkative; he'd usually smile and nod at whatever I said.

There were two main rooms here at this club: the more mainstream room with the bar and dance floor lit up, and the more underground type of techno. In fact there was a third room, offset inside the second, smaller and more relaxed: the 'chill out room', which is where I come to, skinning up a spliff, buzzing on my first pill. There's a table in the corner, and techno is pumping and changing, and I've just been dancing to the underground music, trying to dance with Judy, and she had her spinners – her poi balls – and I was trying to dance with her, and she wasn't letting me get close, and in fact, Judy's new found friends (various girls in club get-up) were ones with which her frustrations were tacitly communicated. It was me who frustrated her. Wasn't it? Judy would dance alone and make new friends; she loved new friends.

And at the table as I rolled a skunk joint, she'd sit with me, and I'd want to tell her about my revelation. At the end of some pilled up chat, in which I'd tried to broach the topic, she'd finished my sentence and said, "You're bisexual." But that wasn't what I wanted to say. I looked to my right where I saw a man with a beard smiling like Jesus (I tripped on his Christ-like figure) and thought, 'That's not what I wanted to say.'

I walked about the club, having taken another pill, dancing to techno on my own, as you do (you sometimes need to fuck off on your own at clubs), and found myself tripping out on some techno-punk's electric head, as he crunched away to the hard beats in sunglasses and was on a podium next to the turntables, really appreciating the fact of his attitude of passion until I noticed the lump in his cheek, which was his tongue, and which I took as a sign to stop me from my appreciative staring, snapped out of it and danced embarrassedly into the main room.

And I stood smoking a cigarette whilst watching the club move in its special way, and sipped on water, and found myself drawn upon resolve to move back into things, towards the bright white of some dude's white t-shirt, lit ever more brightly under an ultraviolet light, and saw my unconscious manoeuvre, and snapped out of it, and danced back to the chill out room.

And it was Paul, now taking off his shirt, which was white, so that he could have a massage off another random reveller, and that is too gay, I thought, and wandered into the main room and danced, crunching away, with my white Nikes and stylish purple suede shirt, for several minutes, beneath a high structure which was the DJ booth for this room, and soon found myself dancing with two beautiful girls, in club get-up, and they were dancing with me, and my mind turned to a night in their company and, as they danced, the beat changed, and a new tune dropped in, and I hollered my high pitched approval, and the girls danced with me, and the best part was when they hollered with me, and I was the man. For a minute then I was the man.

But then, talk about missed opportunities. The beat

changed and, mind altered, I got overwhelmed. I mean, the girls were beautiful, and I'd made them holler, and we were at the centre. But mind altered, I'd got overwhelmed and I had to leave. I had to go. I had to get out of there.

And then I was in the next room, and I danced and hollered to the deep beats of the more underground techno, and I had taken yet another pill, and I was in the middle of a ring – a circle of clubbers all dancing and hollering with me – and then I realised that the beat hadn't changed in a minute or so, that the dancing and hollering were borne of sympathy, that the DJ wanted to get rid of me, and I had to go! I was already exposed – as an idiot! I had to get out of there. I went to the chill out room and hollered, to sympathetic hollers, and as I sat down, Judy was there with a new found friend – a beautiful blonde girl who was introduced to me – who I couldn't even look at she was so beautiful. Her face was that of an angel; her body a supermodel's, and I couldn't look at her she sent my mind into a frenzy, and to make things worse she behaved like she wanted to get to know me... *me*! I looked to my right and calmed down on a face there; the bearded face of Jesus. I calmed down.

Of course, at this time, the new drug was ketamine. Many had sworn to its benefits, but having failed almost every test of administration to all drugs including speed and cocaine (but not heroin or crack), I'd vowed not to bother.

The revellers here began to peter out eventually, and then only the few desperate stragglers remained, and we'd worn out the night, and it was coming to an end. We found ourselves outside the club in the morning light, and I think I was relying on the Jude to get me back home; I wasn't very aware where I was. Judy had found new friends and was going back with them. Strange. I'd wanted to take her home. I'd wanted her to take me home. I'd imagined a nice shower, a spliff, bed. But she had found new friends and was going with them, and I wasn't allowed to go; there was no room in the car. As I walked back past the club the revellers looked at me with disdain, sadness, disappointment.

Somehow I managed to find the train station, but it was one with about twenty platforms, and I was on about twenty pills, and I eventually found the right one. And there, as I walked up the steps, was Paul, and he was sitting with two men I'd never seen before. The first was a bearded man, just shorter than average height, with a baseball cap and downplayed club clothes: brown overcoat, baggy trousers. The second wore a beanie and smiled a lot, and they introduced themselves to me. The three were on their way to Twickenham and invited me back for a cup of tea. On the platform the bearded man (Jack? Tom?) was talking very intelligently, very wisely and cool. So I said I would go back for a cup of tea and the train arrived and we went on our way.

Jack and his friend were on ketamine. "KET-A-MIN!" he'd insisted, addressing my bubbling brains, with a poignant expression. Paul didn't say very much; he never did, but Jack was very entertaining to me, being that I was still high on ecstasy, yet he was very insightful. He talked about some night out with people I did not know, and lay back in the warm seat and addressed his friend (Bill?) and Paul and I. And he asked me, "Do you go to many clubs?" When I said yes, I do, he said, "Yeah, I seen you around." When he said, "Have you ever taken ketamine?" I said no. Then he said, "You need to."

If he'd had any with him, I'd have taken it there and then. But he didn't, yet I was convinced. I needed to take ketamine.

I didn't go back with them to have a cup of tea in Twickenham then: I'd got paranoid and got a different train home, but there was a nice cab drive home from Golders Green. I mean, he really cheered me up, that cab driver. I'd felt so terrible up till that point and I remember the peace of finally going home in the warmth.

It was six in the morning that I was home, and my grandfather was just about to leave, from a week's visiting. Mum was up; she said I should say goodbye to him. I was so fucked I had to blank the old guy. It was all I could do. I went to my room, rolled a spliff, lay in my bed and tried to rest with a million confused thoughts running through my head.

I'm not sure exactly when it was that I did ketamine. I think I picked up a couple of grams from Jude in a Camden pub one evening for five quid. When I did, however, I instantly saw the appeal. In three seconds the idiocy of my hollering was made clear, and lots of experiences now made sense, and in fact, I have not taken a pill since. Pills equalled idiocy, stupidity, happiness at standing next to trash cans. But ketamine was 'down'. It levelled you out. It gave you a ground. And for a while, though it was obvious I wasn't very well, I was happy that my days of taking ecstasy were over.

Triggers

There are one or two good things to being caught up in the mental health system. Admittedly, nobody actively wants to be on benefits, so, at first, when you hear about what you're entitled to, you turn your nose up; you scoff; you say, "I don't need fifteen pounds a week; I can work." For a newly indoctrinated user of services the pay seems meagre. But all around you there are seasoned users saying, "Get your DLA, get your income support, get your incapacity!" and then you find, out of the whirlwind of activity, administration and protocol, you have a nice little flat with heating and furniture, hours every day to watch TV or read books or drink tea or do whatever you want because you're signed off work, and a few extra quid in your pocket. And the way it works is, if you're that way inclined, they make sure you've got enough to get off your face once or twice a fortnight! You only have to make sure you take your pills and see your psychiatrist once a month and listen to your community psychiatric nurse. Despite the adjustment to this situation you can have a pretty sweet life, and that's a good thing. I, however, used the position I was in to secure a place on a college course.

It was an access to humanities course and it was the length of a year, and it was in a college set in a leafy part of a nice suburb, and it was nice. You could go in four days a week, meet students, meet tutors, talk about lovely topics, write about lovely topics, and it was a great place to study. I met many great people, and after a year, I passed the course. I was in to university. So much for hospitals. So much for medication. So much for mental illness.

During that year, it is true, I had stopped smoking weed and stopped drinking, and I even managed half a year without smoking cigarettes. Throughout the whole time I only had to take one day off due to me forgetting to take my pill in the morning. Other than that, the entire year was perfect. And then for some reason, perhaps as a way of celebrating, I decided to have a smoke of marijuana. It was a roach end that my best buddy Gary had left in the ashtray, and it sent me kind of loopy. That very evening I took out my acoustic guitar and walked about the streets of Colindale singing Leonard Cohen songs. The next day was the award ceremony at the college, where students were given their certificates and were applauded by each other. I was too tired to go.

In any case it was the end of the course and the beginning of summer and I vowed to study particle physics, as a conceptual 'primer' to the cerebral and open-ended subject I would study in university, philosophy.

That vow never really came to fruition as I hoped, during this time. Other things decided to occur, as I've mentioned before, which were the events of my fated week's trip to Wales which left me, for whatever strange reasons, somewhat mentally traumatised, and my fleeing to New Forest in a failed attempt to recuperate. But soon I was at the end of that summer and it was late September, and university term time was begun.

As I say, many times to many people, I always reflect on my short days in this environment; largely on a daily basis even all these years later. I remember a feeling of great accomplishment, as I perched at a desk by the edge of a lecture in epistemology, and remember feeling how glad I was to have come this far. Yet I knew even then it was early days for a journey such as this, and nevertheless ventured to work my absolute hardest. Although my time at Harrow College is something I see through rose tinted spectacles, I reflect that toward the end I became perhaps dissatisfied at the feeling of its being merely a bureaucratic institution as opposed to a place where one might learn for love of knowledge, and think for love of thought. So it is, I imagine, I went into higher learning with a sense of anti-bureaucracy, and, I imagine, this was a cause of conflict with such an institution. I guess I couldn't cope with the mechanisms, the dynamics, the internal structure. Being a freshman in unfamiliar surroundings is possibly enough to affect anyone, especially one with such a fragile mind as mine, and the environment was bad enough. But the real test was the stress of the day each student was to register. It was frustration made manifest.

Sent to Hertfordshire's technical campus, the new students were made to line in queues, that extended off in their hundreds, to pass over identification and other papers, then wait in other lines to register on computers, then wait in still more lines for further administration, to pay costs, to enter details, the list went on. I was a mature student and I felt the commentaries and discussions of the younger types around me most grating. They would, to someone with such a fragile mind as mine.

Finally I was set free, able to infuse my lungs with quite the most delicious and necessary cigarette I've ever smoked. There were many stalls set up around the campus with student groups encouraging freshmen to join them. I remember receiving many looks of perplexity as I went from table to table, for perhaps I was not one of the brightest looking of them all. Yet really, I only wanted to find where I may relieve my bladder, and I think I finally found a restroom, and was thankful. And was thankful to go home.

Hertfordshire, bless your soul! But things got no easier. Your "Street", while a clever and inviting idea, which was a vestibule so modern looking one might think himself at some polytechnic (which once it *was*!) was in fact the bane of my entire time at your institution. So full on most occasions was your "Street" that a great attitude of arrogance was developed by your members, that it was like unto a sort of chicken coop, or summer festival ground, where intellectual tacitations were passed most frequently and fervently, and yes my head was still suffering the trauma of my summer excursions. In short, my mind took a turn, certain synapses in my neurofibres got terribly tangled; I lost it. Yet was it in a good way? Something being 'switched' in my cranial centres, one day I found myself in the heart of an experience that nobody would sniff at, a least if they were men.

For one day, as I collected my tray of food and a coffee from the counter in the refectory, I looked up to find the entire tribe of customers in the vast seating areas, predominantly female, to be quite purposefully and literally staring at me. Every eye in the place that belonged to a lady glared at my face with a look that suggested my aims in attaining at least some mode of higher thought had come to something. I had done it. I had surpassed my own expectations of the goals of thought, and through the activity of my mind, had entrapped the entire female population of the university in my head. I looked about with the sense of revelation that perhaps was felt by Socrates at the Oracle, and did a little dance! I then took my tray and sat at a nearby table at which was a young Japanese woman trying to eat. I tried to talk to her, yet her manner was cold. There the experience was done.

It's hard to recollect the exact chronology of events

leading up to the time I now wish to describe. I can seem to remember feelings of distinct alienation, though, and never really feeling like I had been accepted. Images come to me here and there, of certain cheekiness in my behaviour – approaching students I didn't know and making a nuisance of myself, of even having a nice conversation with new people, and one in which I'd decorated a bus stop entirely in sycamore leaves whilst waiting for a bus that wasn't coming. It took me two hours. In any case, such was my confusion, borne of an over activity of a fragile mind such as mine, that one day, in a dark November night, thinking it to be the right and good thing to do, I made arrangements to commit suicide.

Sitting on my bed, looking through some recently taken photographs of my family, I noticed the familiar (yet imagined) sense of relief on their faces, as I told them internally of my frustrations, sorrows and plans. I was so sure I was going to 'do it'. I made sure the flat was spotless – I tidied and cleaned every last corner. I fed the cat, remembering to leave enough food for several days. I put on my CD player the absolute saddest music I could find, thinking that I would eventually be found to the song "Hand on your Heart", the Jose Gonzalez cover version, and I put it on repeat. And I knew that if I was to write a suicide note, it would be a long explanation of everything, and in the end I'd not want to do it. So I wrote the shortest two sentences, I wrote: "Dear mum, dad, Ryan, Corina, I love you so much. It was nice to be at university and I'm glad I made it there. Love, Daniel." And I ran a bath of lukewarm water, left the door on the latch, stripped down to my boxer shorts and I climbed in the bath. I remember my cat Sony, a black thing, a great companion, was up on the side looking at me as if to say, "Wot doin'?" and I said, "I'm going away, Sony," and I looked for a razor. But all I had was a Gillette Mach 3, so I tore it apart, and I was crying, and it came apart in these three tiny bits, and I breathed, and took one and began to make little cuts down the length of my wrist. And I tell you: hurting yourself is fucking hard. I thought blood would gush. It didn't. I managed several shallow lacerations, and was then very suddenly overcome with a deathly sensation that went all the way down my spine, and I looked up at the tiled walls of the bathroom. And I imagined the result of a successful suicide attempt, that it was me, sitting in a bath, facing the tiles, there for eternity, for the rest of time. Hell. I remembered the rules from the film Constantine: People who commit suicide go to hell! And then I snapped out of it. I got out of the bath, wrist bleeding, and I called my mother and told her, "Mum, I just tried to kill myself."

One thing I noticed that evening, as I was back in my old bedroom in Mill Hill, and one thing I will always remember about my mother, is that no matter what, no matter how shitty I can be, whatever I go through, whatever I put her through, my mother will always be *my* mother.

She had driven to my Colindale apartment, and seen that I'd cut myself, and seen that I had packed a bag, for time in a hospital, for I had thought such conduct is the premise of a stretch there, and I imagined that I'd stay on a ward for a while, and draw pictures. And mum took me to Barnet A and E where, after some time, my injuries were patched up as best as they could be, and we drove to the local psychiatric unit so that I could be assessed.

We sat in the lobby of Dennis Scott Unit for many hours. Mum was tired, and I looked at a book I'd brought called "The History of Western Philosophy" by Bertrand Russell. I showed off to her the speed with which I could read: I said, "Mum, see this page? I just read it!" but I hadn't taken it in at all, and mum just smiled peacefully from the soft red chair as I watched her in her patience.

And eventually the crisis team arrived. They were two nurses, Marie and Nadia. Their investigations proved to be positive, if positivity is the assessment of wellness, despite my distraught tears and pleading. Their resolution was that I be referred to the occupational therapy program for a few days, such that I was not to be admitted.

"Why were you crying?" asked mum with concern as we drove to her house. I couldn't tell her.

Mum looked after me very well at that time. I stayed in my brother's bedroom. He was at university himself, and I contemplated leaving university. I didn't know if

I wanted to leave, or if I even had it in me to leave, but I thought about it. Mum would bring me breakfast and tea, and in all my thoughts of leaving, I realised, that lady is a fucking genius!! Whatever I go through, whatever I put her through, my mother will always be my mother.

So I spent a few days living back at home. During the days, I would go to the occupational therapy groups where I would do art, listen to music, watch films and basically try to chill out. There were some discussion groups too, in which one of them I'd meet, among various other people, a young lady called Delilah to whom I was able to relate about our treatment as mentally ill people. She's an African girl who lives in the area and I sometimes see her at a coffee shop. She's a Jehovah's Witness now. Anyway...

After a few days I received a letter from the university that said I was failing philosophy and, suddenly, I suppose having been bored by therapy, I felt the desire to go back to the university.

It was a Friday when I returned, but it was obvious I wasn't well. There were two modules, epistemology and philosophy in film. We were studying the meaning of life and friendship in Aristotle's Nicomachean Ethics. I was pretty sure I knew that the meaning of life was meaning itself, and I remember on the Friday going in we had to watch 'It's a Wonderful Life'. During the presentation I suddenly became aware that I was the only man alive and everyone there was just my plaything, which became an annoyance to one lady in particular whom I prodded continually in the back, thinking it my right, and inwardly laughing because she could do nothing about it. But she turned around and told me to stop.

I was also on an English literature module (I had taken on far too much for my capability) and was studying plays and Shakespeare. It was approaching my twenty eighth birthday. I had been working on an essay about Othello. I was coming to finish it on the day we went out as a family to celebrate at a local Chinese buffet.

I was very unwell at the buffet, and my parents knew I was unwell. And I had a heaven in my head that I couldn't reach, but it was there; beyond understanding.

And while I worked as hard as I could, I also had that said heaven in my head, which I needed to attain by compulsion – a desire. Yet university did not get easier. In a certain philosophy lecture, one in particular about intuition, the lecturer asked the audience what their definition of the idea was. I'd read whole books about intuition, so when the question was asked I reflected on the most influential, by Kant, called 'Critique of Pure Reason', and made to raise my hand. The professor chose me to answer. I knew that Kant had called intuition a concept of the pure understanding, but although that was what I had wanted to say, I put my hand down and shook my head. The professor urged me to answer, and I shook my head again, yet this time he pressed me. And I wanted to say that intuition is a concept of the pure understanding but I got nervous and, in front of a hundred students, I blurted, "... a concept..."

"Common sense, yes," continued the professor in a way as to both save the fluidity of the lecture and embarrass me, by his clever correction of my response which wasn't clever, to those most immediately near me. I felt humiliated.

Some seminars may or may not have gone as well. We had to study 'A Heart of Darkness' by Joseph Conrad, but I hadn't read it, and 'The Woman in White' by Wilkie Collins, but I hadn't read it, and 'Brave New World' by Aldous Huxley, but I hadn't read it. Tim, the mature student, laughed at me for not being up to date with the reading.

The nights were getting darker, and I resolved to stop taking my sulpiride so that I could speed up the pace, and keep up with these several genius youths.

The nights were getting darker, and I found myself in that darkest of dark realms, my bedroom in Colindale, December 2006.

Lobotomy

"You've been a stupid boy again, haven't you?" said my mother, as she sat looking most seriously, with her handbag on her lap.

For all its sterility, the interview room appeared large and colourful, the yellow and orange curtains with their floral designs complimenting the red chairs and blue carpet. As I said, I'd been here a whole day and was hoping I would be able to go home. I sat in a chair opposite mother, and there was a low table between us. "Can we go home now?" I asked mum.

"Daniel, this can't go on," she replied. "You've been behaving strangely for months now. We're going to wait for the doctor and see what he says."

"Mum, I'm fine," I said.

"You're not fine, Daniel," she said with an exasperated shake of the head. I shrugged and looked at the yellow and orange curtains.

"Look. Mum. I'm okay," I reasoned. "I just had a little fight with someone, and he won and that's it – I'm okay, I'm fine! Can you take me home?"

Mother gave me a look so stern I began to feel an ominous sensation of panic ran up my spine. "We're just going to see what the doctor says," she argued.

"Mum, there's nothing wrong with me. I don't know why you can't see it?"

Just then the door behind me was opened, and two men appeared. One was a middle aged Indian man, and he was carrying a small beaker of clear liquid. The other was an older white man with a bald head and a suit, and was a portly size. The second man was clearly the doctor, and I looked up to him with wide eyes and with an expression that tried to say, 'It's very beautiful in here. In fact, it's quite trippy!' The doctor seemed to read my introduction and, quite noticeably and disgustedly, shook his head, as if to say, 'I don't like you already!' This was ominous enough and it caused me to remember the female social worker from my last crisis meeting. I was taken aback, and attempted to adjust my demeanour to account for such an unsavoury first impression. The men came in and took their seats, and the Indian man placed the cup of liquid purposefully on the small table there.

"My name is Doctor Anie," began the bald white man. "I'm the ward psychiatrist here. And this is Raj. He's one of our psychiatric nurses."

Raj smiled, with eyes behind which betrayed a strange and unsettling amusement, about what I would never know, and he said hello.

"Now, I'm to understand that you have been behaving very oddly recently, according to your notes," said the doctor.

"I'm really fine," I retorted, as I noticed two brown marks on the doctor's head and how they were brought out by the bright colours of the curtains.

"You were brought to us by police who said you've been fighting on the street," said the doctor. "That's not acceptable behaviour, is it?"

"Well," I answered. "It's an occupational hazard, I think. Many different things can happen on the street, and having a fight is just one!"

"That may be so," the doctor continued. "But I hear you've also been fighting with your brother. That's not acceptable behaviour, is it?"

It was true. I'd had a physical encounter with my brother. I'd been searching for a Grandaddy CD I knew he had borrowed, and was brought to a sudden frightening rage when he didn't give a fuck, and pounced upon him to apply my angry discipline on his person. In that instance, having been trying to sleep, Ryan had jumped out of his bed with a panic that was accompanied by squeals of fear and, though he was younger than me by eight years, he defended himself well and none of my blows connected.

"Yes, that's true," I said to the doctor. "But brothers fight all the time." I told him about my best friend Gary's brothers who were always in vicious battles with one another. The doctor sighed.

"We believe you have disordered thoughts, Daniel,"

Doctor Anie put forward. Mother was nodding her head in agreement. "We'd like you to take this medication."

The fact was I only wanted to go home. "Mum, seriously?" was my appeal. "Can you not just take me home? I'm fine. I'll be okay. Honestly."

"Daniel," mum addressed me. "Something has to change and you know it. It's been going on far too long. You have to take the medication."

Now, I did not know what the medication was, or what it did to you. In fact, I imagined it to be a mild sedative that would make me somewhat sleepy. But I did not ask what the effects were, not did I think to. I had other designs. In fact, my resolution was that one way or another I'd be walking out of here and home this very night. I tried to stall for time, knowing that I had got out of situations before and, though it seemed impossible, I would get out of this one.

"Well," I sighed. "How long will I be on the medication for?"

"For one year," claimed Doctor Anie.

"One year?!!" I gasped. It seemed a very long time.

"Then a review," said the doctor. "Will you take it?"

It certainly was not my intention to. In my mind I started to imagine the beginnings of another altercation.

"Mum," I appealed. "Please, just take me home and I promise nothing else bad will happen. I'm okay, I promise."

She looked forlornly at her lap and shook her head

despondently.

"Daniel..." she sighed.

I had resolved to go home that night and was stalling badly for time. No matter what the effect of medication I was adamant I did not need the stuff. After some more minutes mother had to go. My last chance at escape was walking out the door. "Please will you take the medication?" mum pleaded. "I have to go, but I'll bring you back some cigarettes. What do you want? Silk cut?"

And she left.

And I was in the brightly lit interview room with Doctor Anie and Raj, and they were going to try to convince me of drinking the pot of clear liquid. My options were running low. In truth, I was becoming a little bored.

"I know the problem," I began in address to the two men. "You know, I know why I've been so angry." The two men seemed interested. "It's because I'm homosexual! I've realised!"

I was sure that was the problem. I continued to explain my position, that a lot of anger had built up as frustration, that I was psychologically fixated on my denial of my homosexuality, that that is a common feature of many problems in society. I explained that men were unable to face their sexuality, because they are conditioned, and you should understand this.

"You should understand this," I explained to the two men. "You're both men of genius!"

And they laughed. It was a reluctant laugh, but it was clear. I was making headway, or so I thought.

"Still," said the doctor. "We'd like you to take this medication."

It had been a good forty minutes having this same discussion, and I was becoming restless. "Look," I said with an air of levelling with them. "What will happen if I don't take the medication? Will there be trouble?"

"Yes," nodded the doctor. "There will be trouble."

I imagined the altercation that might ensue: more hefty looking nurses dragging me around and causing me pain. The small pot of clear liquid was in my hand. I was tired and bored now, and all things considered – what's the worst that could happen? I'd be a bit sleepy. I'd feel a bit sedated. It would be a bit like a dose of a hash spliff. Besides, these people have been very nice to me today, and I can't deny that. And I only want to go home, and I can't see any other way out.

Actually, in retrospect, in the world in which time travel is possible and you can return to those moments of concern, I would have continued to talk to these men. I would have talked and talked, and we would have discovered that I am a nice guy, but that I'm just misunderstood, and we would have figured everything out. I would have walked out and gone home, in retrospect. 'What's the worst that could happen?' I thought, and then with another thought, the one that has been the bane of my life, the precursor to each and every mistake I've ever made, the two words I said before I started smoking, before I left school, before I took ecstasy, before cocaine, before everything, I thought, 'Fuck it!!" and downed the liquid.

It was a little bit like my head was smacked with a tonne of bricks. It was like my soul was suddenly sucked down a black hole of shit. It was like my mind was extinguished by a shower of Domestos. I couldn't even think. I couldn't even think I couldn't even think. I couldn't even complain that I couldn't think. I could then see that these nice men had just done something to my brain that my brain can't understand what they've done to my brain because the part that could have understood what they've done to my brain was now extinguished, and I couldn't understand, and couldn't understand that I couldn't understand.

I shot up from the seat, and now Raj was standing, and now the world did not look so bright and clear, and it looked like a grey and empty room and it looked flat; two dimensional. Raj was standing and still had this expression of amusement on his face, and I wanted to hit him. I wanted to punch him. But I could not. I had realised that that shock to my system, of this foul tasting chemical substance that was like the worst, most horrible sterilisation liquid that you would not even put on your knee if it was grazed, I realised that that shock was exactly the type of thing that would warrant an attack on its administrator. But the effect would make me so docile I couldn't even feel the anger. In retrospect, I would lamp Raj and smack his grin from his face.

As the power of natural emotions began to drain from my heart into nothingness, I became emotional and helplessly did my utmost to salvage myself, and grabbed a pen from the table, and wrote in my book that I'd brought in, and wrote 'Don't ever forget this! Sue them! Hate them!' And all the while I was yelling out, "WHAT HAVE YOU DONE TO ME? I'M GOING TO SUE YOU! HOW COULD YOU DO THIS? YOU CUNTS!" And I was crying because I could see my thoughts disappearing, but they were forced tears; I was trying to salvage my thoughts. I was shouting. I was yelling. Raj was smiling, and now I'd got the attention of the nurses outside on the ward and, as I shouted, they came in and began to draw me out into the hall. "YOU FUCKING ARSEHOLES DON'T KNOW WHAT YOU'VE DONE!" I cried desperately. "I'M GOING TO SUE YOU ALL!"

A female nurse held me by the arm, and I was taken into the dining room, accompanied by two or three other nurses, and I was calmed down but still crying, or trying to cry, but really wanting to giggle.

I had lost. For all my ability to get out of other situations, this time was not one. I had lost.

I sat then at a table and, still teary eyed, put my head in my arms and closed my eyes. The tiniest of tiny little electrical impulses jumped digitally from the synapses in my brain as though my mind was a circuit board, yet that was all I could see, and it depressed me totally, and the sight was meagre. On top of all this, my brain now was hurting; it was a pain as though my head was in a vice, and my brain was cramped by its grip. Eventually I glanced up.

Life was continuing as normal without me. The nurses had gone back to their duties, the patients on the ward were milling around suspiciously, and then I noticed something. That strange air, possessed by each of these patients that made them seem decidedly odd to say the least, that same strangeness that made all these people seem acquiesced to docility, well, it now made total sense. They had each been administered the same chemical substance that I had, and that was the reason for their odd demeanour. And now I was one of them.

The world was turning upside down. In that dining room, with walls covered in posters, the symbols on said posters appeared to shift about as though arrows realigning magnetically north. The world was plain, and this medicine was anything but an LSD trip, but even then the world seemed as though it was actually returning to normal, and I giggled. I giggled as arrows pointing one way became directed in another, and the right way. And I giggled and cried and, though my head hurt, I knew this change would be permanent. I'd never get my thoughts back. This seemed funny to me. It was anything but funny.

Mum had been back and had dropped off my Silk Cut. A nurse had passed them to me. Entering the smoking room I watched the other patients, who no longer faltered under the power of my previous nonmedicated state by which I could see who they really were; I now could only see who they thought they were.

These men walked around cockily and macho, demanding cigarettes or lights from cigarettes and seemed hostile. Even the older man with grey hair and glasses seemed full of bravado, as if his thin frame and blue cardigan were enough to strike the very fear of Zeus into my heart. I knew at this vision I had no hope of helping him, or any of the other men there, into the light of the flame of truth about who we are. Not anymore. As the evening drew on I sorrowfully smoked cigarette after cigarette while various characters floated in and out of conversations with me in which I was enlightened as to my initiation into this new world. "You sit there, you take your medication, you get out," somebody was to tell me.

I finally was shown to my bedroom and it was a far cry from the pictures in my imagination. There was a window, a sink, a cupboard and a single bed with a white sheet. The wall was scratched with a degree less imaginative graffiti than you might see on desks in history class at school. I unpacked my things which were in a bag that my mother had left me, and which included a CD walkman and some CDs. I began to play a CD by Frank Black and sat on the bed wondering how best to kill myself. The only way to do such a thing was to kneel before the door whose handle was a metal cylinder and smash my face into it. I was sure that would cause me a great deal of pain before it would kill me, so I went to sleep instead.

Avon Ward - Day two

I awoke at seven or so the next morning, having been caught trying to fuck the bed, by Ahmed whose face was one of disgusted horror. I was told to get up and go for breakfast and Ahmed left the room. The medication had not only damaged my brain but also my libido. In fact I was surprised that I was able to achieve an erection at all, no matter how weak. As I pulled on my jeans, Meena was standing outside my door giving orders to someone down the hall, and I thought about giving her a glimpse of my penis, then thought twice. I sat on the bed.

A small bald Italian nurse came in with a pot of clear liquid. "Medication time!" he said.

"I don't want it!" I whined, now all the wiser as to its effects.

"Oh, you don't want it?" he said.

"No thanks," I said, waving my hand.

“Ok, suit yourself,” said the nurse, and he walked away.

‘Was it really that easy?’ I thought. ‘If only I did that yesterday.’

My head was in pain. Well, my brain was. But also my jaw ached and stung; it clicked as I tried to chew my Weetabix. The dining room was half full of patients, and the staff, whom I now realised were psychiatric nurses, milled about between tables. The shutter to the kitchen was open; a nurse would serve tea and toast to order. The trolley with the trash basin was in the corner. Across from me was the Irish patient, called David, who was stuffing spoonfuls of cereal into his mouth and making a great mess of it all over the table, and I winced with disgust and a hint of humour.

When I was done I went to ask a nurse to light my cigarette. This nurse was an attractive young woman with an Irish accent, whom all the patients fancied. She had a lighter in her hand but then, rather than spark the cigarette with it, she proceeded to place it in her top shirt pocket that was right over her pleasingly large left breast. ‘Strange behaviour,’ I thought, then smiled as I assessed the reason for it. ‘She wants me to reach into her top pocket so that she can report me to the authorities for sexual misconduct. Very clever,’ I thought. Yet she was not able to pin that crime on me, no. I asked again for a light and she took it out and I was sparked. ‘The cheeky bitch!’ I thought.

I wandered from room to room; from smoking room

to bedroom and back. There's not much else to do on the ward other than that. And my head was painfully tense, and I walked from the bedroom and became aware of three or four rather large men in blue t-shirts and jeans gathering in the hall. They looked like builders and certainly weren't patients or nurses. At the entrance to my bedroom's wing a man approached me. He was older, with white hair and skin. With an Irish accent, he introduced himself as a hospital manager. "How are you feeling today?" he enquired.

"Very, very angry," I answered with a grimace. I wasn't. In fact I was trying not to appear too amused and was actively and deliberately trying to seem as angry as I thought I should be under the circumstances of the events last night. The hospital manager went away with flighty importance, and I went over to stand with the large men.

"You look like you've been working out," I mentioned to one of the shorter, stockier men, by way of starting a conversation. He said something under his breath in an Irish accent, and I was slightly confused. Just then I thought I could smell a fart, and blaming the short, stocky man, I walked away into the day room. My head was painfully tense as I took a seat in there and, for a minute or two, took in my surroundings.

After a few moments my serenity was interrupted by the appearance of Ahmed at the entrance of the day room. He seemed larger than life as he filled up the doorway and I noticed his hands were in medical gloves.

"Daniel," he began as he glared into my eyes, with an ominous hostility that was tinged with apology. "We are going to hold you down and inject you because you didn't take your medication this morning."

I was shocked and my jaw dropped accordingly. I was standing by now and began to search about me for a way out, but of course by now I was used to losing. The day room was about twenty five feet long, and I ran helplessly to the back of it. There was one doorway that led onto an outside space but it was locked. Next to that there was a square window that was open but only did so to the measure of two or three inches. Nevertheless, as Ahmed approached me, I tried the window and rattled its handle, yet with resignation whined, "No..."

Ahmed grabbed me, but I didn't put up much of a resistance. Yes, I struggled, perhaps out of his grasp at one instance. But then the four Irish men must have got involved, because I was lifted off my feet and dragged into the hall of the ward, shouting. "FUCK OFF!!" I shouted. "FUCK YOU, YOU ARSEHOLES!!" And then I *did* put up a resistance and began kicking and yelling, but to no avail. The large Irish men now had my arms and legs and held me down in the middle of the hall of the ward. Now, physically restrained, I only had my mouth to retaliate. "YOU FUCKING PERVERTS!!" I yelled at the greatest volume I could. "YOU FUCKING WANKERS!! I BET YOU'RE GETTING PROPER THRILLS OFF THIS AREN'T YOU?!! FUCK YOU, YOU FUCKING DIRTY CUNTS!! AARRGH!!"

I was on my front, my body was restrained, and their plan was to inject me in my buttock, but I had a belt on.

"He's got a belt on!" someone said.

It is in fact the case that their decision was to break the belt by yanking from either side, and soon they had ripped down my jeans. I yelled and shouted, "PERVERTS!! THIS IS YOUR JOB, IS IT?!!"

The next thing I knew my backside was jabbed and I felt a familiar disappearance of thoughts and an influx of chemical docility, but, since it was familiar, it wasn't as bad as last night. I was exasperated, as the men lifted me some more, and I was carried further down the hall to the room in which I was left when I first arrived here; it was the plastic room, and they call such a place 'the seclusion room'. I could smell the plastic as they dragged me in there. The men held me down, and with the kind of conduct that is the reserve of policemen and dangerous criminals in a cell, they left at once. I turned around to see the white haired hospital manager slowly closing the door. With an instinctive impulse, I tried to get up quickly and escape. But the manager slammed the door, locked it, and peered through the small window, then went. I had lost again. And to make matters worse, I was, in fact, locked in what I now realised was the rubber room. In earlier times this type of room would have padded cushion walls. Today they were made of plastic. There was a plastic covered foam chair, and there was a plastic covered foam mattress, and the room was about ten feet square, and there was a high and tiny reinforced window near the ceiling, for light, and there was a ventilation shaft to its right.

After five minutes I was investigating the shaft for weaknesses, standing on the chair, and noticed its cover was fixed by screws whose heads were designed with two small holes, rather than a cross, and wondered what would unscrew them. Realising my jeans' zipper tab would do the trick I tore it from the main metal part and tried to undo the screws.

"Get down from there, Daniel!" said a voice behind me. It came from a speaker in the upper corner of the other side of the room. There was a security camera pointing at me from behind a circle of glass. I got down anyway, it being a fruitless endeavour; as if I was going to escape through a ventilation shaft!

My head was painfully tense, and I lay on the blue plastic covered foam mattress and wondered, as much as my mind would allow me to wonder, what in the fuck happened in my life that I ended up in the padded room of a psychiatric hospital.

****

They left me in the rubber room until evening, for what reason I'll never truly know, and let me out after dinner. They fed me with something they had kept aside for me – some meat and vegetable dish – and I was afterwards able to go and watch television and smoke.

Television programs did not look the same since yesterday, in a weaker and less immediate way. I quietly mourned the loss of amazing looking television, along with its meaningful dialogue which now seemed hollow and one dimensional. In fact, everything around me lacked any recognisable beauty whatsoever. I'd never seen a world like it. Objects had no form now, whereas before they were full and three dimensional; I remembered the way they would marry with their counterpart ideas of the mind, and be thick and whole. Yet even the memory of such philosophical nuances was unavailable to me. Even the faces of people looked sunken, shrivelled and ugly, and I was unable to see anyone's inner spark. It was as though I'd died and gone to a false world of dull, lifeless people, and my head was painfully tense.

Soon it was visiting time, and mother had arrived with fruit and other things: a book, some paper. I was expected to converse with her, but I really had nothing to say other than to complain about my treatment over the last day or so. I still didn't know where I was, relative to the local area, other than inside a locked mental ward, and lacked any sense of orientation whatever. Yet, questions which lay previously unasked at the back of my mind were now finding their way forward. Why was I here? How long would I be here? What was going to happen to me? What is that stuff they keep giving me? Mum was still concerned: in a sense I was blaming her. She just told me not to do too much, that I should take things as they come, ride it out and everything will be alright. "Do what the doctors say," she said. It was an annoying and yet curious feature of circumstance that my parents had arranged to go away for two months to Samoa, where my father had land, and they were leaving over the next day or so. The alternative proposal was for my mother's best friend Carrie (Auntie Carrie; mother of Steve, my childhood friend) to come in and visit me each evening. And also marked down for visits was Joe, a friend of my father's, for whom we'd worked before. My head was so tense and I complained that I had lost the ability to think – worse – that they'd given me brain damage! That was exactly how it felt, and I found it unbelievably difficult to empathise with mum's concerns – and worse! – to add to this, she didn't look very good; sunken and hollow and lifeless like everybody else. She had to leave, and I struggled to muster the compassion to care what she did.

The evening drew on and soon it was medication time. This time, I knew better than to refuse it. I approached the counter where Meena was organising the doses. I had several questions to ask. "What is this stuff?" I queried.

"Sulpiride," she answered with office. "Antipsychotic."

"What does it do?" was my next question, coming, I realised, one day too late.

"It takes away your thoughts," was her reply.

"Takes away your thoughts?!" I exclaimed despairingly, shocked at the presumptuous preposterousness of the existence of such a substance.

"You want procyclidin?" she asked.

"What for?"

"Side effects," she said.

"Side effects?!" I exclaimed despairingly. "What about the actual effect? Isn't that bad enough?"

I acquiesced to the programme of medication, totally dissatisfied with everything life had to offer. I repaired to the bedroom and tried to draw some picture to somehow regain my hopes.

Months ago I'd rekindled my love of art and drawing, and half-made plans to return to college and study it. The world around me was full of beautiful and psychedelic things, and I was inspired, and particularly by television documentaries about the British greats, or architecture, or Indian floral designs. One documentary told of the way that all buildings were based on the phallic representation, and so tonight I remembered that and drew something phallic.

The phallus was to become religious church windows, stained glass, and lacking any real inspiration. I listened to a Richard Hawley CD for a while and I thought about Glastonbury Festival 2003. I thought about the feeling of community, and togetherness, and tribal thinking. And I thought about escape – again – and I heard someone shouting, and it was a girl's voice, and I heard more shouting, and it was a boy's voice, and I thought about escape... And then I heard distant smashing glass!

From such a sound I harboured the idea that Avon Ward, and indeed the entire population of this institution, was in the process of a revolution! And it was a revolution of escape. 'How did they smash that window?'

I thought. 'They must have kicked it in,' I resolved. I wondered how I'd do the same, and remembered that the style of my footwear was a leather walking boot, and judged that if I stood in a certain position, and aimed correctly, I could have that window out in seconds.

But was it a revolution? How would I know? Answers were found in my investigation into the goings on in the hall on the ward, and when I peered out and saw every staff member gathered in the dining room, discussing some issue or other, it appeared that they were trying to say, in their own surreptitious way, "What are you still doing here?"

That was my cue! I ran inside my room, jumped up on the wide window sill, and started booting at the glass with directed kicks, and it smashed, which got the attention of one of the night staff who ran to the room only to witness me kicking the crap out of this window.

"Daniel!" she cried, just as the pane gave way, and I managed to deftly and skilfully perform a dive any ninja would have been proud of, out of the window, and then went into a military roll just clear of the broken glass, into a bush in the garden.

The rush was incredible. I had escaped. I was free. I ran without looking back, as far and as fast as I could, and consequently arrived at a high and barb-protected fence, which there was no way of being climbed. I was in an enclosed garden – enclosed by walls on three sides, and this bastard fence – and I was stuck contemplating my situation. The situation was dire. The light from a flashlight was shining at me. "I can see you!" called the voice of an African woman from a second floor window.

The nurses from my ward had not given pursuit: the back door to the garden remained locked, and I darted about the small area for inspiration. There was a barbeque structure, and I thought I could hide there for some reason, and that was one of my options. Actually, it was my only option other than to climb back into my bedroom. After a moment's thought, realising that, if I wanted to, I could even stay out here, and that not only had the staff not pursued me but in fact seemed to have forgotten about me altogether, I climbed back into my bedroom. There was broken glass around the edge of the pane, and I cut my palm on a piece, and the cut bled, a splash falling on the sill.

With bashful regret, I sidled into the hallway of the ward and was met neither with anger nor disdain, but with care and concern; that attitude I most appreciated. I was still excited with the rush of adrenaline, as I was escorted into the seclusion room, which was the rubber room, which is where I was to try to sleep. Before I could do such a thing I was interviewed by the night doctor, and he probed my thoughts.

I told him about my revolutionary notions, having resolved to blame my action on that sense of communal liberation which I felt was the order of the day, prior to its execution, rather than the mere frustration of the stress of the last few days. "So you thought that everyone was escaping, is it?" summarised the slight and young doctor.

"Yes!" I confirmed, to his placation, and my surprise at his placation, which placated me in my fears of further altercation. The latter never happened, and I consequently fell into a hopeful sleep.

I was in the day room the next day when workers were brought in to fix my destruction, and as they came in and got their first glimpse of it, I felt a deep sense of amusement when they took it in and chuckled to themselves at this perfect image and subtle irony of the mess I'd left.

Yet my head was still painfully tense.

After Before

And the rain came down.

The crisis team drove away down the road, and I went back into the house and resolved to find new accommodation somewhere different from here. I went up to my bedroom to pack a bag of things – clothes, books – and by the time I'd come down my dad had walked in from work. He owed me some seven hundred quid, and after I told him I was leaving, he was able to find it for me. I said goodbye to them both and caught the bus to Edgware.

I knew that my treatment of the services was quite severe, that that was not the end of it, that I would soon be receiving a visit from police, and that I had to go. Though I had no sense of an outcome – whether prison or worse – I knew I had to go.

With that seven hundred pounds lining my pocket and feeling like a traveller about to go on a big journey, I stopped off at a pub in Edgware to drink a pint and think about my next move. Some sports channel was blaring from the corner of the room. Some builder types would come in and engage in raucous banter with one another. As a barmaid cleaned out the ashtray on my table, I stared out the door and wondered about finding a room at Gary's house where his family kept a bed and breakfast. I resolved that it would be too close to home, and after a short while, that I should like to find some room above a pub. I imagined myself in a job at one of these houses and thought about the possibilities of this new life. I finished my pint, and remembering just such an establishment on the route to Watford, left the pub and caught the 142.

Having got off at said establishment, I went in and enquired about a room. The barman said there were no such rooms, so I left and continued on to Watford.

Night was falling when I alighted at the 142's terminating stop, and I walked down the first road I saw, and it wasn't long before I saw a house with a sign that said

ROOM TO LET. CALL 07********* TO INQUIRE.

So I phoned the number. A man named Scott spoke to me and was there within fifteen minutes to show me the room. Some preliminary steps later, including a phone call to my father for a reference, and signing of a contract saying I'd pay seventy pounds a week, and handing over six hundred pounds as a deposit, I had secured a room.

It was totally unfurnished with not even a bed (Scott promised to arrange that), and that night I used my jumper for a duvet and my bag for a pillow. But at least I had the room. After reading a few paragraphs of a philosophy text book, I turned out the light and fell into an uncomfortable and disturbed sleep.

The next week or so were spent familiarising myself with the area. I now had very little money and some days I walked up and down roads visiting construction sites to ask for work, to no avail. At one stage I had found an advert in the paper for a position at a jewellers as a typist, a job which I was able to do, but was asked to complete three weeks without pay due to my lack of credentials, so I didn't take the position. Mum put up the money for my first week's rent. Meanwhile I would walk around Watford town centre, and surrounding streets, and found myself befriending the local homeless constituents.

During the course of the week my father had brought several important items to the bedsit: a television, a stereo, my guitar. One day I took out my guitar so that my homeless friends could enjoy a song, and I wandered the town happily playing Suzanne by Leonard Cohen, and other songs, even making some up as I went. Some of these people really enjoyed it, and so did passersby, but it never occurred to me to busk for money. However, my friendship with the tramps of Watford was short lived, for one of their members took a distrust of me, and one night at the underpass to the north of the centre, I felt I was better at a distance from them and walked away. I still had no money.

There was a convenience shop on the road where I lived, and despite befriending the owners there, sometimes I would pinch cans of food and other things. I didn't want to, but I had to.

Some days I was able to secure work, however, at a site run by my father, which was back in Mill Hill. The world looked very beautiful then, but I was alienated by my inability to behave very well, and found I couldn't cooperate with other site workers. On one occasion I had got angry with Steve, who was working there, because of the way I thought he was treating my brother, who was also working there. But the fact of his mistreating Ryan was just a paranoia of my mind. Nevertheless, I had a fucking go at Steve – shouting and threatening – and I forever soured our friendship that day.

So some days I had a few extra quid. One thing I enjoyed to do was frequent the local internet cafe and write emails. Sometimes I would write them to friends. A friend of mine, Sarah, a previous crush of mine, was away travelling the world, and we'd communicate that way. But mostly I'd write emails to myself. I enjoyed typing. And I'd go in chat rooms – in those days I would go in the Yahoo religious rooms that were still in use – and talk rubbish to the Americans.

One evening, writing an email to myself, three girls were at screens to my right and they were each very attractive to look at. The one closest to me was engaged in writing to her father, as I could see when I peered over her shoulder and caught a glimpse of her screen. She was laughing with the two other girls who were her friends, and I noticed one or two spelling mistakes and

I resolved to boldly interrupt the young lady. "Excuse me," I said. "I just happened to glance at your email there and I hope you don't mind but I couldn't help but notice: you've spelt this word wrong, and that sentence there should have a comma in it just there. It seems like a very important email, so I thought you'd like to know!" And I corrected the misspelt words and, although this young lady went a little quiet (perhaps at the embarrassment of her lacking of correct grammar and so on, perhaps at an uncertain sense of an imposition on my part), her friends were most impressed by the confidence and ease with which I approached them. In fact, when they had finished their work in the internet cafe, they smiled admiringly at me through the window from the street outside as they walked away.

The good thing was I had figured out a way of approaching women in internet cafes! One Friday afternoon, among a room full of customers, there was quite the loveliest young lady I had ever seen, perched at one computer, doing whatever work it was she was doing and, although I tried to restrain myself, that became a failed endeavour, and I went to sit by her and pointed out every mistake I could find with her work, even ones she was making as she went. Unfortunately for me she had a very protective friend who shouted at me very angrily that I should sit somewhere else. In fact, such was my embarrassment that I left the cafe altogether.

I would go to pubs, when I had enough money, and usually sit at the bar and write or watch the patrons, and listen to their discussions. I must have felt at home in pubs, for their familiarity, and trusted people. One day I thought I'd put my wallet on the top and address the surrounding strangers, "Can you look after that? I'm going to the loo!" Then I went to relieve myself, noticing my level of tipsiness, and when I got back to the bar my wallet was still there. The patrons were giving me the oddest looks. I finished my pint and went out of the pub. When I checked my wallet I found twenty pounds was gone. Then the odd looks made sense, but they were right; it served me right and I accepted my idiocy.

That night I had a dream. For ages I would dream of parties. I would always be at the centre, dancing and hollering and getting everyone going. This time the party was at a Mesopotamian temple and thousands of people all dancing to techno and surging this way and that. They would move like the tide up the temple steps, and I would holler happily to their reciprocal cheers, and they would surge towards me. There was the temple and thousands of revellers all hooting and hollering and dancing, for no discernible reason. And they would move and surge, and now, by proxy, at my whim. And I was a central feature in this dream, where every clubber at the temple surged towards me, and confused by their very own joy (which spoiled their joy), produced Scott. Scott was my best mate in dreams, yet here his face was full of concern. As I whooped once again, and was crowded once again by the crowd, Scott pinched my right testicle.

And although I was in a dream I felt a great and real pain there, such that I had to wake out of it. When I did so, the pain in my nut was extreme, yet subsiding. The pain was a dull sting, as only a pain in the nut can be.

Every so often, and quite persistently, I would get a call on my mobile from the local police station asking me to drop in; I wasn't in trouble, they needed to check up on me. I told them I was fine, but they insisted they needed to check up on me. After a while I stopped answering their calls. As a result the police had found where I lived, and by questioning the local residents, had located me at home one day.

I wasn't in trouble, they said, but it was related to my outburst at the crisis team that time. The two officers, a male and a female, listened to my explanation – that I had felt the crisis team had been personal with me, and wanted me to go to hospital, but I felt fine, and I felt put under by their request so that's why I shouted at them, but I'm really fine, I'm okay, I promise. The officers were happy with this reason, and that I was not in any danger or a danger to anyone else, and left me alone.

My ankle was sprained. In the first week I had found the local hospital and, whether I was registered or not, one of the doctors had provided me with a crutch. But for whatever reason, on days of wandering the area, I found myself hanging around in the waiting room and talking to patients here. I don't know why; perhaps

I was waiting until somebody noticed me, perhaps because it made me feel calm and relaxed. In any case, at times, I could be made to feel useful.

There would sometimes be a patient in need of reassurance or a friendly word of advice. On a bright day one day I noticed a very distressed looking young woman sitting in the waiting room almost close to tears. "Are you okay, love?" I asked. Her shoulders became hunched, and she looked to her feet. She began to sob a little. I imagined that she might have been diagnosed with cancer or some other terrible affliction, and said. "Don't cry love, you'll see the doctor. They know what they're doing!" The young woman burst out in tears, and I sat next to her and put my arm around her to console her. She continued to weep, and I thought, 'Aw, she probably needed a good cry,' and I felt like I had done a good deed. She was called into her appointment eventually, and I waited for her. When she came out she walked right past me – no thank you; no nothing.

In any case, I would still hang around the hospital grounds. It made me feel better.

Watford has a church, and one Sunday I resolved to go along. In fact I'd been in town since earlier in the morning, in particular, at a coffee shop, where my latest revelation was to talk to the coffee shop girls. I had ordered a cappuccino to go and said something like, "I know it's early in the day but you should probably drink one of your beverages. It'll stop you looking so tired!" And it pissed her right off! She scowled at me with her tired eyes and, as I chuckled to myself about how annoyed I'd made her, I noticed I had amused everybody who was drinking whatever beverage in the shop. A man walked in, and even by the very sight of me in my humour, gave me a helpless grin, as though he had seen the entire situation. I went out to sit at a table in the morning sun and drank my cappuccino.

In fact, at this time, my main preoccupation was to find a female partner. I had discovered several great techniques for gaining their interest. For example, perhaps the day I lost that twenty quid by my own idiotically trusting of strangers, I saw quite the loveliest looking brunette specimen making her way through town, as though heading back to work from her lunch break. She passed me, and after a moment's thought, I turned around and sought to pursue her. She was sat at a bench when I caught her up. The technique I would use to chat up this ambitious seeming and power-suited delight was to start by saying the exact opposite of what I would suggest that she say. So I said something like, "I think it's okay to treat animals badly."

"I don't think it's okay to treat animals badly," said she, concurrently having fallen into my trap of saying exactly what I had planned, by doing so.

"Yes..." I smiled whilst rubbing my hands together conspiratorially.

In any case, my pulling technique had not worked because, in the real world, women are free and spiritual creatures with minds of their own, and this lovely thing had to go elsewhere.

But there at the coffee shop that morning, I was becoming desperate. There was a nice man in the forecourt of the establishment, at a table, and three frankly stunning blonde ladies at another, and I quite fell in love with one in particular. The nice man, a Mediterranean man of sorts, exchanged a glance with me in which we shared our appreciation at these ladies, and beckoned me to sit with him. We spoke of the loveliness of these amazing women, and I recollected that I was unable to look at them because, by their appearance alone, I would become turned on. My stomach churned with the desperation of my own need to acquaint myself with the lady of my designs. And soon, in the light of my ignorance of the face of opportunity, and lack of any words to say, my heart dropped into my shoes when the ladies decided to leave. I resigned myself to acquaintance with my Mediterranean friend, and when I finished my coffee I said goodbye and walked to the church.

I went in. There was a full congregation, and I could only find a seat at the very front. An old pastor was talking and soon was introducing a younger one who took the pulpit and began a sermon. His topic was some moral issue from the bible, something about the absolute truth of free will, and I, being a man of somewhat philosophical bent, felt a pang of disagreement that I could not help but pipe up and say, "But do you really believe we have free will?"

The young pastor was livid. His face utterly reddened, and he shouted at me – *shouted* - from the pulpit, "DO NOT INTERRUPT ME WHEN I'M TALKING!!" Needless to say I was very much put in my place and reluctantly fell silent, yet seethed with embarrassment. The young pastor continued his sermon and a person from the congregation approached me and said, kindly, that questions should be left until after, when we have coffee in the rectory. I sat for a moment, understanding my mistake, then, after a while became overcome with a religious sorrow that made me feel like crying. I nearly did, too, but since I was so embarrassed and I didn't want to give these people the satisfaction, I stopped myself and walked out. The congregation wore faces mixed with amusement and self-righteous superiority as I did.

In any case, the whole event led me to feel a great desperation – both sexual and spiritual – and I went home that night, back to my bedsit, and started to shout at God. I mean I *shouted!* It wasn't praying, but it was born of frustration, and I yelled out, "WHAT'S YOUR FUCKING PROBLEM?!!"

The night before my second rent day I had gone to a pub nearby to sit quietly with a coke, a half pint for which the landlady charged me a pound. "A POUND?!" I exclaimed in shock. "Fuck it, I'll give you *two!*"

I sat quietly there at the bar, gazing around at the mostly empty room, and saw a group of men of varying ages who were accompanied by a very good looking woman. After some minutes the woman was ordering drinks next to me, and I struck up a conversation in which I found that she was a nurse and liked witty men. We spoke for the duration of the period which it took for her order to arrive, and then she went back to the group of men with a sense of disappointment, and I realised soon that she must have been in a relationship with one of the younger ones, who in any case did not seem to be paying too much attention to her.

When one member of the group produced some kind of large piece of electrical equipment, like an oversized current detector, I reflected on the options of the form of the situation in hand. Perhaps someone had brought said item in to show off its high-range technology to the rest of his friends, it being a fairly modern thing. Or perhaps said item was being waved about, as a subtle warning of the danger of getting into an altercation with these men, that they might beat me with it. Their concern at my bellicose manner was not entirely obvious, but on occasion I made meaningful eye contact with one of them. He would mutter under his breath and get back to his drink, having recognised my fearless and dark demeanour.

In any case, I became bored and walked around the other side of the bar, visually assessing the thick and full depth of the of the decor in the pub: the deep dimensions of the furniture, the bright and glowing lights of the gambling machine, the psychedelic hexagonal appearance of the yellow and orange patterns in the carpet, and in my head, mentally offered everybody in that pub out for a fight. Nobody took me up, though, and I left and went back to the bedsit.

I lay on the bed and masturbated about the thought of having sex with the lady in the bar, and I came and it was good, but it wasn't enough. I needed a woman's touch. Not yet ready to sleep, still feeling the frustration and stress of neither fighting nor fucking, I sat upon the floor of my room and began to write in my notepad.

I had taken out this pad to draw churches in the area at different times during the past two weeks but none of the drawings turned out any good. I had even drawn a representation of my best friend in dreams, Scott. Tonight, with my pad on my knees, I looked outside the window at a street lamp and could see a swarm of wasps buzzing viciously around its light. Occasionally, one wasp would fly to the window, apparently to try and tell me something. "We can see you," perhaps was their message. In any case I felt their attraction to electricity was somehow mirrored by my own spiritual and mental power, which was at the height of activity. And I began, in misplaced frustration, to write a hate letter. It was a hate letter to God. To God!

And it was a hateful thing, full of swearing and cursing, anger and spite. And I would say every hateful thing I could think of and address it to God. And I didn't hold back.

During the course of writing it, I would hear occasional strange sounds, seeming to come from below my window at the first floor, that were a subtle source of confusion to me, yet of which I took no immediate notice. As I was writing, the sounds would come sporadically – a crunching, or the clanking of glass or cans – and I started entertaining notions that there could be people outside, perhaps the patrons to whom I had shown aggression in the pub earlier. Yet my hateful letter continued.

Eventually, I had done and I had written a long letter of spite and hate to the heavenly Father, through my anxieties and frustrations, and by now the sun was coming up, and I finally looked out of the window and saw a huge pile of black bin liners full of trash heaped up directly in front of my dwelling. There were hundreds and I gasped.

This was a personal attack! My fears were realised! I was locally hated! My heart went into palpitations, as I realised that my conduct in the area over the last two weeks had the result that all the members of the community of the Watford area that I had annoyed, or started on, or somehow wronged, had dumped their household crap right on my doorstep to wreak revenge on me. So I phoned the police. I complained about the horrid occurrence, even telling the lady I was having a heart attack by it, but in the end she hung up on me. In any case, it was a panic attack.

So the day now being rent day, I vowed that I would not pay it. In fact, I spent the day in the library seeking some legal help from law books, that I might be entitled to any compensation or the rent be legally waived.

In the evening of that day the landlord's wife knocked

on my door to collect the rent. When I told her I would not pay and why (that the neighbours had left a huge pile of rubbish out front) she told me, "That's where it's supposed to be put," and she called her husband. Scott arrived, and I had locked them out, but they'd had a key, and I was told that tenants in the building had made complaints about me shouting and making them scared. And when they eventually decided I would have to be evicted I begged them to let me stay. I pleaded that they let me pay, however, it was too late; I was being evicted. Suzanne by Leonard Cohen was playing on the stereo when Scott called my mother, and she was not surprised, and she drove to me to collect me and my things. And Scott put our mattress in his boot and drove back to mine. And I rode with mother in the car, back to Mill Hill, and perhaps from the adrenaline of such an altercation, I couldn't help but turn the notion in my head, 'I'm a genius! I'm a genius!' And we arrived back to the family home, and Scott took off the mattress and returned my deposit.

I was back home again.

This is not the promised land...

Verily, I begin this chapter at a much, much happier time when it was some July evening in the year 2002, and I lazed on my bed in the topmost room of my house, which was my bedroom, and rummaged through assorted papers and books there, that were drawings and various attempts at writing; mere paragraphs of surreal imagery which many of the previous weeks I had spent collecting. Verily, I say unto you, I began immediately to feel a subtle yet strong sense of emotional freedom or spiritual contentedness there in that room with its sloping, triangular ceiling and blue and white painted walls, such that I had never felt the likes before. I breathed with calm serenity.

I reflected on the previous weeks and at the wonder I felt in the strange beauty of their course, which was like the course of my rebirth, a period of liberation from the strains and pressures in my life before then, and

I got a sense of someone arranging things, that someone, somewhere, had laid a plan, and I was being led to some end they had organised. I reflected on that day when, tired from my first night of sober unrest that was borne of a revelation (that men and women were soon to evolve in the structure of their romantic relationships; there would hence become three to an affinity – a male and two females, or a female and two males), and having spent the entire day drawing pictures and watching closely the development of events on the news – a feeling of change and circumstance; an impending happening – I was gripped, and would puff at Silk Cuts, with fascination. Something was going to happen.

Verily, I say unto thee, something *did* happen. For during a documentary on the history of the people of Mesopotamia, and an exposition of their culture and writing, I was made aware that the allusions to Middle Eastern genius were seemingly and somehow directed at *me*. The deep aqua blue of the stones; the reference to bubbling tar-pits; the identifying of the Mesopotamians with a rich civilisation; and the revelation that among them were arithmeticians like that other famous genius, Archimedes, these ideas were in phase with the frequency of my head's understanding, and I responded through emotion and cried in tears of happiness.

I reflected that I had to have been one of a handful of similar types, as I held my fist to my head and could see across the scope of the Earth at this time, and could see that I was at the heart of a great event. I felt an affinity, borne of the designs of the British media, which I since and for some time had grown to trust despite youthful and rebellious prior reservations, and although still shrouded in the puzzling uncertainty of the future, was relieved and satisfied in this new experience. When I opened my eyes the world was vastly different. Edges and patterns of designs on images in this beautiful and secret show stretched and flattened as though I had come up on some psychedelic trip that must have been stopped up in the boxes of my mind, for that sort of thing is the premise of fiction and imagination, yet it was real. Now not only did the television's images seem more lucid, yet so did the world around. It was with joy that I went in the adverts to go to see my mother.

Verily, I say unto you that my mother was drinking a glass of red wine whilst some play blared out from the radio that she listened to, and I went into the dining room where she was and I saw to my left, on the corner of the room there, the large indoor plant that looked lovely, and as if I had never seen a plant before in my life. "That plant looks nice," said I, as I stared at it in amazement.

"Thank you," said mother, who perked up as though the compliment was paid to her.

I wanted to tell mother of the glory of the recent revelation I just had, and did, yet I said it with the least tact, and said, "Mum, I think I'm a genius. The television just proved it to me." But this made her concerned.

"What are you talking about?" she said. The frustration was clear and I couldn't find a way of explaining. I had gone back upstairs.

I sat down on the couch in my room to watch more of this television and see what else I could learn. My Silk Cut had long run out and that was good since I thought now an excellent time to quit. But somebody was coming up the stairs. Earlier I had arranged that Gary visit and, although I would have been happy to have seen him, I knew he would bring cigarettes, and possibly marijuana. The bedroom door was knocked, and I went to it. Yet it was not Gary. It was my mother and she had tears in her eyes. "Daniel," she said as though saying goodbye. "Are you okay?"

"I'm fine, mum."

Mum hugged me and told me a story about my uncle Mick and how he got sick many years ago, from a similar circumstance, and how hard it was for the whole family to cope. "I don't want you to get sick, Daniel," cried my mother, and we hugged and cried.

"I'll be fine, mum," I promised.

****

Verily, I say unto you, I felt fine as I lay on my bed going through papers and books, and it was getting late, so I decided to rest my eyes. The feeling of sleep was beginning to take over, and then, just as I slipped away into dreams, a great crack of lightning and immediately a burst of thunder woke me with a shock, from directly above my window. I looked out to see an effect and saw an elderly couple who lived across the gardens also looking out.

I was awake now and thought I would stay up for a short while longer and I moved to the couch and put on a CD of sad songs (such was my mood) that were recorded from the internet, and listened.

It is hard to explain what I heard when I listened, and there may be no way I could truly ever do that, but I had an affinity with each song on there, that began with Out of Reach by Lowgold, and it says, "There is no coincidence," and like the message that came with the lyric, "When I try to breathe, breathe," I was lifted, and I breathed. And then To Sheila by Smashing Pumpkins came next and I was made real, by the chorus, and it was as if I could not believe. And then was Suzanne by Leonard Cohen and, for the second time now, I was so touched that I cried in tears of happiness at the beauty of the lyrics and the images of the garbage and the flowers there, and I looked around and I saw the beauty of the world, for the second time. And there indeed was something in the way, when played Something in the Way by Nirvana, and yet what it was I did not yet know.

Verily, it came to pass, that I was reading some culture magazine, by name of The Face, and saw in the pages therein that there were great coincidences within the sentences, and I read some of the paragraphs and was followed in thought from paragraph to paragraph, whose content could never be copied to writing, such was the depth of coincidence and thought, such that it came into my mind, that maybe some science was at play;

that maybe some scientists were somehow at the root of the accuracy of the coincidences between the words and my mind. Yet, it being that such a sentiment proved utterly beyond my understanding, it was that I forgot about that one entirely. And it was good, yet I turned the magazine to the couch and picked up a book (of all things) that did lie there, and it was, to be sure, Keep the Aspidistra Flying by George Orwell, and began to study the words and the nuances of duplicity in coincidence and, losing all thought and consciousness of it, did drift away into serenity and peace. "Hello!" came a voice from the sentence that I read. I gasped in alarm at such a thing of originality; such an effect as I never had seen. And verily, I say unto thee, the voice spoke again. "Do you know who I am?"

Suddenly the events of the last few weeks made total and complete sense and I answered, with relish, shock and joy, "You're God!"

It was obvious that it was! Because who else would it be? Who else would introduce themselves in a book? Certainly, it was God! And I read further a few sentences and I got the impression of a long and intimate conversation in which the Heavenly Father Himself would say, "It's lovely to meet you!" Yet I imagined that such intimacy would be reserved for the famous, and I was not yet famous. "Where am I?" asked God. It was a question I knew the answer to, it being that His Holiness' omnipotence had been a subtle subject of inquiry of the last few weeks.

"You're everywhere!" I proposed with the glee that comes with certainty.

"Yes," He said, and I became thoughtful at the idea and began to look at things around the room for evidence of his presence. I looked at the television which stood on the tabletop, and then my gaze drifted beneath the tabletop, at the collection of VHS tapes I had accumulated over time, and it fell upon a particular title that was The Spy Who Shagged Me (that one with Austin Powers), and I began to zone out on the video, and momentarily became doubtful of the truth of God's omnipotence. Yet I relaxed, and just as that doubt nearly made itself manifest, the mist cleared, the words slotted into place and God jumped out and said, "Shagged Me!" It was a droll exclamation in the manner of one having been caught in some act or other – hiding, I imagine.

And then I jumped up and I was amazed because I understood now; I understood everything – it all made sense. I had just met God! Now I was out of my seat and going round the room to explore this notion, that I had found God, and this idea of His being everywhere. I picked up some other book and flipped to a random page. "Here too!" said the Lord.

With disbelief and excitement I looked about me and dashed over to a shelf, where there was a CD case for a compilation of rock music, and picked it up and examined it. "EXCLUSIVE!" said the Lord with sarcastic wit, as though the fact of his existence and manner of appearing was old news. Yet I was fascinated still. Here was the oddest nuance about life, a secret known only to a few, and I had discovered it! I went to the other side of the room and looked curiously at a cutting pinned on the door. Yet this newest oddity in my life was not immediately apparent, and a second or two passed, and then God spoke again, "Information, information, information," and I was relieved and placated, although I sensed the tired out tone of this greeting, and I calmed myself somewhat. I went back to sit on the sofa.

I wished to try to have this conversation, which in the back of my mind I ached to have, and resolved to pick up another book. I do not remember the particular book but that, as I settled down to read it – to converse – I found God had gone back into hiding; was not immediately present. I continued reading nevertheless and soon it became apparent that He was talking to me and in the process of describing Himself to me. At the point which I thought he would be going to admit He is a genius, he said, "I'm an idiot!"

'How strange,' I thought, 'that the Heavenly Father should call himself such a thing.' Lord, I wanted to say, Lord, you are no idiot! Don't say that! Please! You're a genius! But what I did instead was to sort of shrug my shoulders vacantly and say, "I think I can see what you mean."

The internet was relatively new in those days. Lots of people were buying PCs, and my family were in that category. Dad had bought a Dell computer a month ago, and we were just getting to grips with it. I had gone ahead and uploaded my entire CD collection to the music library, had set up a music streaming account with Audio Galaxy, and randomly searching Michael J Fox news, found myself on an American posting site called Unsolved Mysteries. It was in the days before Facebook and Twitter and those other social media sites had taken off, and I thought I could have a laugh as an anonymous user who would just take the piss out of the other members on the site – trolling – by use of my British sense of humour. The first post I wrote was something along the lines of, "I'm going to go to the doctor to get liposuction for my pig!" In any case, USM would turn out to be quite important to me, if only for the fact that these fifty or more people were there for me. Tonight I decided to go online and post about this latest event – that I had met God – on Unsolved Mysteries. I imagined the reaction of all the 'USMers', how I would post and be the most popular man on the site with the most to say and the best, most exciting life. Yet I got downstairs to the computer and went online only to find, from some technical glitch, I wasn't able to access the website. It was a half-formed thought, that I could ask for assistance from a Yahoo chat room, but it was way back in the recesses of my mind, and I gave up and went to go upstairs. "You tried!" said God cynically, from the midst of a sentence on a page on some letter on the table in my view. In my heart I knew what he meant: I had not tried.

Yet, presently, I was in my room again and I had picked up a copy of the Holy Bible and had resolved to begin to read it in its entirety. I lay on my bed, and God was talking, and I was becoming used to his messages and signs in the form of the word. I began to think about how the bible was written by people who had also had this same encounter, and it all began to make sense.

Yet, though every effort was made in the endeavour to quit, I had a small lump of hash left over from the last few days and was thinking how I could make a big deal of going somewhere romantic and religious to smoke my final joint. A plan developed in my mind to climb to the top of the hill at the local open space, listen to God, and make it my last.

God is everywhere, and God being everywhere He would be in songs. Having pulled on my sneaks I collected my walkman and chose a tape to put in. God being everywhere, I resolved to choose not music but a cassette that was called Learn to Speak Spanish, because why not? And I went on my way.

Verily, I say unto you, that it was the case that the world was full of beauty and easy on the eye. I must say that the first things I noticed were the paving stones at the edge of the pavement at the junction I had first to cross and what I noticed was their shape and angles and how they swept around, low to the ground, and looked almost unreal, and more and more very much like the memory of a play set that I had in my childhood. I crossed the junction and the Heavenly Lord began to talk about some very general things, and the topic turned to a friend of mine, Ron, who I had recently been hanging out with. "What do you think of him?" asked I to the Lord. I thought there would never be a chance of a direct answer; I was still in a state of disbelief.

"Aburrido!" said He after a pause, which is 'boring' in Spanish. I chuckled a little and continued walking as if to say, 'I think I know what you mean!"

God continued to lecture in bouts of Spanish and English, some of which I understood, not because I knew Spanish, but because the messages behind the language were obvious. I came to the gate at the open space and went through. The dewey field was fresh with the scent of morning. God was talking all the time; all the time. He was making jokes and being very funny. He has a very good sense of humour, does God.

Back in my bedroom I had rolled up a joint and when I arrived at the top of the hill I sat on a bench and smoked some of it. The sleepy feeling of hash stonedness descended upon me, and the clarity of the evening's occurrences started ebbing away. The sun was coming up over the horizon, and it looked to be a beautiful day and, when I had finished half the joint, God told me, "Put it out!" I obeyed reluctantly, yet impressed with this manner of instruction, and stubbed the spliff out on the bench. "Now repeat after me..." went the discourse of the tape, and we both said with understanding, "ABURRIDO!"

I smiled at this little piece of beauty and stood up. In the back of my mind I heard a tiny voice that said,

"Try weed; it's much better!" I continued to walk and went over the hill and went to make my way to the other side of the open space.

Lo, it came to pass that the Lord would try to open me up! As I walked on the other side of the hill, down past the trees and toward the opening to the next field, God would say, "Be free!" and tell me to free my arms and gesticulate in the campest way.

"What if someone sees?" I said, that being my main concern. Although it was not yet five in the morning I thought I could see a dog bounding about in the distance, and dogs always have owners. Yet it was but a large magpie. I did try, to open myself in the way that was suggested, but it proved so hard, and perhaps I was still not sure of myself.

I went left towards the path that went near the local boy's school. There was a ditch, of average depth, on the far side of which there was a stile that led onto the school grounds. I stood on the near side, awaiting instruction. "Do you want me to jump the ditch?" I asked. It was too crude a way of requesting something from God, and I did not expect a reply.

"Ci!" said the Heavenly Father with authority, and I was nonplussed.

"Can't argue with that," I said and jumped the ditch, and now I was going to go into the field where the boy's school was. But then I imagined all the pupils looking out from their dormitory windows and laughing at the queer! So I explained this to my new friend who was fine with me if I wanted to walk the other way. I did so and came, eventually, to a gap in the trees on one side of a path and, thinking it to be the way to a certain field that was in my mind, I went in.

I went in and had to hack down various branches to get through to a part on the other side that looked like an opening but was blocked by brambles and plants. 'I could try to get through here,' I thought. 'But it'll take some work.' I was on my knees, pulling plants and branches out the way. When it proved a much bigger a task than I thought, I resolved to come back out of the opening and find a different way. "Weak one!" said God, in reference to my Christianity. Actually, the Spanish lesson had just got to the end of its first instalment. Nevertheless it was a clear indictment of the poor impression I must have made on our Lord God, the Heavenly Father. I resolved that it would become my life's priority to become strong in character and belief.

I walked on, through dewy fields, and saw several images in my mind as to various possibilities of a definite goal to this, my first walk with God. One was that I seek a particular field where there was another hill I was familiar with and another bench that I may sit and think with God. Not before going past some of the places, where Kelly and I used to fuck in various clearings and spaces, did I get to that place which was in my mind. I looked about only to find I was mistaken and there was no bench. There were only some hay bales and a skip. Yet though the morning was fresh, and God's word was bubbling in my ears like an aural Jacuzzi, and such things were being said, that to relate every sentiment would be impossible, I viewed this field and said, "This is not the promised land."

And I imagined the tribes of Egypt going over the desert. And now the sun was slowly warming up, and I thought what a journey this walk could be, were I able to go to the end of the park and down past my old junior school, down the road where Steve, my best friend in childhood lived, past there and to the cafe at the roundabout down there, where I might have breakfast. And, although I had a vague notion to trust in the Lord and go to that cafe, I did worry, for I only had about a pound to my name and you cannot eat and drink for free. Yet, the thought being in my mind, I went down to go through to the far side of the park where there was a different entrance.

Verily, I thought about the times when in youth I would frequent this open space with Steve and his stepfather Terry and sometimes their dog Sally, a lovely black thing that would bound about the trees and fields with stick in mouth. How we would explore. We would find branches, which made for good walking aids, and sometimes a bivouac built by some poor homeless person. I remembered something Terry once said. "England is the best country because we have all four seasons." He was full of wise sayings, was old Terry.

I had gone round a bush nearing this other entrance of the park – there was the beginning of a tarmac path that led to the other entrance – and at the corner was a dog shit bin. "Wait!" God said, in whatever the Spanish was. "Look at this."

"Yes, it's a bin," I said with a tilt of the head.

"What do you think of it?" God would ask.

"Well... it's rubbish isn't it?" I would answer.

"No!" cried the Lord with a hint of exasperation. "It is beautiful!"

I stood in wonder and amazement at this dog shit bin and smiled as if to say, "I think I can see what you mean." I walked on.

And I walked down the tarmac where some of the planted trees on the right had plaques at their bases, and I was able to see the entrance gate, beyond which was a red car parked in the road. Now, the Spanish lesson had just been discoursing about a red car – in particular, a red Volkswagen Polo. Now my mind was tending to elaborate a certain coincidence that went: 'If that red car up ahead is a Polo... well, wouldn't that be something!' It wouldn't be lying to tell you that I was fairly sure that it was a Polo. But as I finally clicked through the gate and got a closer look at the red car I could see it. It wasn't a Polo.

Now, I think God was able to sense my feeling of slight despondency as to this small failure on His part, by not performing this particular miracle of coincidence. Therefore I was mightily cheered when I looked to my immediate right, and there was in fact a Red Volkswagen Polo and this was coincidence enough. At least, it was a lovely insight into God's mysterious ways. How that red Polo did shine to me!

Now, I say I went right, which was the way to go back home, thinking I was quite tired anyway, but I really should have gone left and down to the cafe at the roundabout and seen what might have happened. I wonder and always wonder what sort of life I would have now, had I that degree of trusting innocence. My life would be very different. That walk would have been some hike, and may have been many miles, yet my wish was to make my way home. I did that, now on the road which was not a long road but on which I learned that I was 'slow', by the sign painted upon the ground, and was never happier to be, and I was nearly home. Yet, along that way, there is another park. It was to my left and I went in the gate as if to compensate for my weakness of character by extending the walk a little more.

As soon as I got into Mill Hill Park, by its rear entrance, I came upon a flock of the tiniest sparrows that were perched on the ground. I approached them with serenity assuming the flock would disperse, but strangely, they remained, and I was able to walk among them as though I was nothing. In fact I stood amongst them, these sweetest of innocent creatures, having never been in such a situation, and looked at each one in the eye – but didn't stare – for if I stared too long at one sparrow it would get scared and make to go away. In fact, my eyes darted easily from one little eye to the next and there must have been forty or fifty sparrows.

I apologised that I was unable to feed them. I daresay they did not mind at all. I daresay these birds were enjoying this moment of calm understanding between species as was I. Thus, I resolved to spend the whole pound in my pocket on bread, for their breakfast, and come back to feed them. There is a shop – an Esso garage – just outside the park and, as I made my way to it, I saw three teenagers leaving a bench in the distance. 'They must have been here all night,' I thought, 'just as my friends used to do not too long ago.' I think I must have scared them away. In the Esso garage I picked up my bread and had a slightly fucked up conversation with the Indian attendant, in which I thought he was talking about my hair but he wasn't, and I left feeling awkward but at the same time hopeful in the realisation that the poor young man didn't know too much English and at least we had tried to communicate. When I got back to the park the sparrows had already flown away.

Now I was very much closer to home – right by it – and reflected on the extent of my walk with God and the fact of its being probably a kilometre and a half at least, and now I was primed to walk; to always walk; to walk everywhere. As I came closer to home, I noticed the English flag in the window at our neighbour's house. Said neighbour was someone, a typical Brit, to whom I didn't say much but now was advised that just a thirty second conversation would be enough – to whatever end: perhaps just friendliness, or spreading love, or just to smooth over any tension there might have been – and I thought I could see what God meant.

The key turned its lock, and I thought of my father as I went inside. He was a lot like our neighbour in many ways; they were men after each other's hearts. And I went in and put the bread in the kitchen, while the tape continued to play, and I went to stand in the lounge. My walk with God was over, His introduction concluded by His final sentiment. "And that's the boss!" went the tape, as a lesson in office conduct was finishing. I mean, it should have finished there; I should have left it there. I should have taken out the headphones and sat down and been glad of my new associate. Perhaps I should have known to do such a thing? Yet, with curiosity and impudence, I continued to listen in case of one more message. "Week six!" said the Lord. Now with the knowledge of my absolute ineptitude of religious strength, I went up to my room and lay down to sleep for some hours.

More Failure

I love my sister. She has always been there. Whenever I reflect on my life, because she is only really a year younger than me, whenever I look back, she is always there. Mum says of course she is, of course she would be, I would not remember a time when she wasn't.

My first memory of her was also the first time, aged two, that I consciously recognised my father too. At Christmas 1980, on Christmas day, I can almost remember seeing the snow on the ground outside the window of our flat. It used to snow at Christmas in those days. Mum and dad had got us a Wendy house, though I'm not sure if it was for Corina or me or for the both of us; this little plastic thing with a red roof. The pair of us went inside of it and marvelled at the space and the fact that this space was ours, and there were windows on each side and we looked out of them. I can remember Corina sitting there in her white petticoat with her short curls of light brown hair, and we loved the Wendy house and we were safe inside.

Then, I went to one window and looked out, and my

security and safety were soon in jeopardy because from outside came a great fucking roar, of what I imagined was a ferocious lion or angry monster, and I cowered in fear and so did Corina, and speaking for myself, I had never known such fear. We screamed, the two us, and went away from the window and over to the other side, and yet there came another great fucking roar! I don't know why I felt so afraid. The imagination of a child must be as vivid and ripe that the unknown is made all the more real. The roaring eventually died down, and with curiosity and bravery, I left the Wendy house and saw that the source of the roaring was a man and that he was smiling. And now he was reclined on the sofa, and I went to him, recognising that this man was my father. It was the first I recognised him. But I had seen this man before, yet only now realised who he was, and I went to him. They don't remember these times, my parents, and in that respect I have a better memory than they do. But also, that was my first memory of Corina. We bonded over the fear of a cruel world.

Growing up with Corina, we had our ups and downs, and yes, I felt protective of her, yet despite my large size I was not a strong person. I used to have to rely on Corina's strength of character and hope that she herself would be wise enough not to fall in with bad people and bullies. For the most part she did that; there was never cause for concern. Growing up and being in different years of the same school I think it helped that I was in the older classes, that most danger was warded off by such a fact. I was always wary, nevertheless, of some particular people who I deemed to be a potential problem and always sought placation from the edgier, naughtier types whom Corina had to contend with, and sometimes I was placated. Yet Corina was never in conflict with anyone – not really. I suppose if I had to I would have defended her happily. I just never had to.

At high school, it was a slightly different story. I was first to arrive there, being the elder. I tried to get on with others as best I could, and there wasn't a great deal of animosity – just the usual shit. Except for this one kid. Kevin Howard.

He was a big black kid. He was in my registration class and he was huge. I hadn't really dealt with black kids much before – there weren't many in my primary school to deal with. It's funny to think of it now: there really were no black kids in my primary school. To be honest, Kevin wasn't a bad guy. He could have been much, much worse, if he wanted. But for whatever reason, he didn't seem to like *me* very much. I mean, he didn't overtly hate me, or deliberately go out of his way to get to me, but I must have tried too hard to be his friend. Such behaviour is always suspect, and he took a dislike to me.

The school had to go on a sponsored walk around the area. We had all gone in our regular clothes, with backpacks that had our lunches inside. My friends were Mervin and Don and Owen, among some others. They were quite cool, and I was sort of a nerd and I didn't mind the company of nerds and I had started the walk with some of the nerds and I wish I continued. Some kids said I shouldn't walk with the nerds so I left them behind. I wish I hadn't. Anyway, I was on my own and I saw Kevin up ahead with earphones in. I thought it would be a good opportunity to make friends with him. I caught up to him and asked him what he was listening to. "The Simpsons," he said.

"Can I have an ear?" I asked chancily.

He paused for a second, as he considered his response, and then moodily said, "No." I think I realised at that time that I was going to have problems with Kevin.

We walked on. I had joined some of the boys from the year. At one stage someone had found an electric fence, and ten of us had joined hands to see if the electric shock would travel through us, which it did, and it was funny to see ten of us get electrocuted at the same time. And I walked with these boys, mainly with Mervin who I thought was a good guy.

Somewhere along the route we all stopped at a bench for some lunch, this big group of boys. I joked around with Mervin and must have said something that upset Kevin who was in the group. I don't think it was anything much – I wasn't even speaking directly to the guy. I probably said something like, "It's unlike you to share your drink!"

Anyway, Kevin turned to me very angrily and aggressively and said, for no real reason, "I don't like you!

Go away!" which was a surprise but I didn't go anywhere. I just stood and looked at Melvin as if to say, 'What's this?'

"I don't like you!" he said again with increased agitation. "Go away or I'll hit you!"

Then it was clear I was in trouble. Obviously, in retrospect, I should have had a fight. I was a big kid, yes, so really I should have stood my ground. But I knew I wasn't strong. I looked again at Mervin as if to say, 'Are you coming with me?'

In the end I realised I wasn't going to have a fight – it wasn't worth it. I reluctantly sloped off and I was miles from the end of the walk, and Mervin didn't even come with me. I walked most of the ten miles on my own behind two girls from one of the higher years, who sang songs the whole way.

Before the end of the first term, mum and dad decided to take the family abroad for a year due to the recession, and we travelled all over the world – to America, New Zealand, Australia and other places. When we came back I found myself in the middle tier classes, whereas I was previously in the top classes. Needless to say, Kevin was in this tier, and I was gutted. However, the lad was not a great deal of trouble to me. I just kept myself to myself. Now, however, Corina was in the school, having joined the year below. I felt sorry for her about that because her entire year was all cunts.

In fact, it was not until the final year that real trouble came. Corina was also in the middle tier of classes, so her group of friends were the more edgy types. And I didn't even know about it at the time, because she didn't tell me, because she knew he was the biggest fucker in school, but she was being bullied by Kevin. Anyway, something had happened; some people had started on her, perhaps after some period of trouble, perhaps Kevin even hit her. I don't even know. Corina didn't tell me. But she had told my dad and one day he came down after school to give Kevin a talking to.

First I had left the gates and seen dad waiting there outside and I'd thought, 'Sweet! Ride home!' Then he said, "Which one's Kevin?" So I pointed him out to dad and dad approached him, I can't remember exactly what was said and I wouldn't want to make it up but Kevin was scared, although he tried to save face by being rude and loud. Dad was intimidating, his finger pointing fearsomely in Kevin's face, but I knew it wouldn't have been right for dad to have hit him, although I would have liked to have seen that. In any case, there'd been words. Dad was still in his building clothes and so Kevin called him a tramp. Dad paused, surprised, and then laughed. I was standing a few feet away, watching, and at that point I realised – now would be a good time to have a go at Kevin... Now I could finally go up to the fucker, see about an attack, have a fight with the fucker and be protected by my dad all the time. I could see it in my mind. I'd lose, of course, but that's fine. I'd just have to go up to Kevin and punch him.

There was a pause; a moment in time where everything stopped. The universe teetered on this moment, like I was supposed to do it – supposed to fight Kevin Howard – the perfect opportunity.

Rooted. To. The. Spot.

The moment passed. My stomach was knotted, and I felt like the biggest pussy on earth. And I knew there and then I would never forget this moment again in my life. I knew I would always remember this as the time I pussied out of a fight with the school cunt who'd bullied my sister and insulted my father. Complete. Fucking. Pussy.

Nothing else happened after that. Kevin walked away, and dad dropped Corina and I home. But I knew where Kevin lived because I had found a list in a teacher's draw once, with the address and phone number of every student in the year. So that night dad went over to talk to Kevin's parents, and the next day Kevin came to school saying that my dad was alright. But I'll never forget that missed opportunity. I never will.

The one where God says see ya later, alligator

I walked with God for eight months. There were so many moments of joy that it would be a full volume to do them justice. The entire time is a moment in itself I reflect on with happiness and a sense of longing to return.

Alan knocked on the door, waking me out of bed. I heard the knock and knew it was him straight away (you know how you can tell who is at the door from the way they knock?). He came up to my room and had brought a CD of his latest demo, and put it on the player, and it was alright. It was a beautiful day and I suggested we go for a walk.

I noticed that the pavement had the same toy-like appearance it had that morning, and as we turned into the park entrance, having gone along the road, I couldn't help but to point out the beauty of the trees to my friend. To my surprise he seemed able to appreciate what I was talking about, yet his appreciation still lacked a sense of awe. I wanted to give Alan that same awe *I* was feeling, and though having struggled mildly about the topic, and knowing in my heart to be surreptitious about the event, I found myself in a brave or stupid enough mood to say, "Alan, I met God last night." The thing was that such an admission had not made my friend yet suspicious of some madness or lying in me, but he was indifferent, and we talked about God, and he probably imagined that I'd meant I had *found* God.

"What scares me," said Alan, "is the existence of Satan. If God exists, then so must the devil!"

"Well, I shouldn't worry a great deal about that," I interjected, "because if God exists, then He is at the top of everything. He is in command of everything, even the devil." That sense of comfort appeased us both.

We arrived at the cafeteria in the park, and I bought a coke (Alan did not order), and we sat on the chairs outside in the mild sun and chatted. A small child came up to us at our table and stood there staring at me, deliberately, for attention. His father was walking nearby, and I purposely ignored his son until he went away. "It's the Queen's diamond jubilee today," I observed. "We should go!"

Alan agreed, so we walked back to my house, where his car was parked, and I went in, and Corina was there doing work on the computer. "It's a beautiful day out there," I said to her, to which she gave me a huge grin.

"Today is the day of the Queen's diamond jubilee, and I'm going with Alan, and it's going to be really good!" Corina smiled once more. It wasn't until I had left the house that it occurred to me to invite her. I thought about knocking on the door to make such a request, but in my heart I knew she wouldn't want to. I went to Alan's car and climbed in. Our plan was to drive to Edgware train station, park, and get the tube into town. We weren't very far along before I thought to drop in to see Gary and invite him with us.

Gary was laid out in bed clothes on the sofa watching Big Brother on his flat-screen. He was quite relaxed, so any attempt at convincing him to join us in London was never going to work. Nevertheless, I would try, and for the next ten minutes went through every good reason why he should come, and every bad reason why he shouldn't, and at times there was a glimpse of hope, but his laziness was too powerful, and Alan and I left for the palace.

It was a great day to be British. The tubes were buzzing with people all talking and laughing. On the way up, Alan explained to me about some business situation that his dad was dealing with, and I was happy to listen. We arrived at Green Park among a massive crowd all here to celebrate the anniversary of the crowning of Queen Elizabeth.

At first we sat on a mound near a tree and nearby two ladies just behind us. As we looked around ourselves, I felt an urge to start a conversation with the ladies, if only to increase Alan's chances of meeting someone, and though I realised how easy it would have been (I even knew what I would say), I did not talk to them. In retrospect, we would have found two new friends and had a lovely time.

Events transpired and, after some time, we moved to walk nearer the palace. Prior to this outing it had been the case that my insularity prevented me from looking in every direction that I might have liked. However, now, and not for the first time, I was able to glance up from my nervous shame and face the world. What I imagined I would see was a world of happiness and ecstasy, but in fact, what I did see was not so happy and ecstatic: the world was stressed out and confused as ever a world could be; they had not seen God's joy in love, and I knew I had work to do.

We walked beneath the trees, along a path where things were quieter now. There was a man on a bench, glaring away from us into the air. Alan approached him and began to talk to him. I wondered if they knew one another. I didn't know what it was Alan explained, but it was of great fascination to me. In thirty seconds, Alan rejoined me, and we walked on. I didn't think to ask him what he said to the man.

The palace was farther on. There was an ice cream vendor this way, and it occurred to me the mundanity of the sight of those waiting in the queue, of which there were at least twenty. It seemed odd how we do things like wait in lines, yet under no authority other than what I would later discover to be the social contract. I forfeited an ice cream, and we continued.

Our journey had led us to the front of the palace, and now there were thousands of people. I looked among them and saw the red, blue, and white colours of the Union Jack being waved, and worn on hats and scarves and shirts, but there was nowhere to stand, no way to get through everyone to see the procession. A tall television screen was mounted at the side. We decided to continue on and walked a path with crowds on either side. I had seen a man perched atop a pillar, with a television camera. He saw me too, and I imagined him turning the device on me. I imagined my face on all British television – the news, BBC, ITV, whatever – and tacitly requested to the cameraman that he ignore us.

There was a grass bank on the left, and despite our not being filmed, I felt a little exposed and was glaring at my feet. I then remembered my world of nervous shame and how now I face up to it. And I did face up to it, and walking by this bank, I looked up, and there were hundreds of people – families mainly – and saw them all happy and smiling. And there was a man: a father, large and bald-headed, sitting happily with his children playing around him, and we looked at each other, and something was exchanged; something royal and special – we knew who we were; he was the king, and I was the queen, and it all made sense. It was a great day to be British.

Alan and I walked on and now decided we would

find our way home. Some access the police had blocked off, so, as a crowd of us sought another path, I noticed the way we would all fall in line. It reminded me of cows. We moved through the streets and then we were at Trafalgar Square, and then I believe we were at a shop that sold water, and I bought some water. Eventually, we found a station and went home.

Back in Mill Hill I fancied a beer, and bought one, and took it to the park and sat with Alan, under the tree we used to sit beneath with our friends not so long ago. I picked at the label, as Alan told me about a new drum kit he had purchased, and I declined when he invited me to play it; I was tired. In the end Alan went home and I went inside to ask God about something. "A lot of people didn't seem to like me when I was in town," I complained, which was how I felt. I was reading a pamphlet about religion.

"Do not go back into the forest," He advised. He was only joking, of course. He was being ironic.

****

Now there were many beautiful days like this, with easy movement around the world, and beautiful surreptitiousness at every turn. I could tell you about them all each in turn, and yet it would come to nothing. I could tell you about how I walked everywhere, and the time I walked The Burroughs to the library there, and how I felt as if I was in a dream, and how at every point of view I was enlightened by a nice thought, or world changing sentiment, in buses and advertisements.

I could tell you how, influenced by the American posting website Unsolved Mysteries, I would write and write, and write until the feeling was like my mind had left its body. I could tell you how I went back to college, and the several occasions that I been centre of attention in class; how the tutor had got in a fluster at his cursory recognition of my genius! I could tell you in great detail of the worse times of my relation with the Heavenly Father – how at Christmas that year I had promised to give my brother's friends a bag of skunk weed, but didn't for being annoyed at them for no good reason, and then smoking that skunk weed myself and having a panic attack I thought was a heart attack. I could tell you how amazing everyone looked; how they were all geniuses and they looked like it. I could tell you every nice thing God ever said to me, and the time I had a major revelation in the night, and came downstairs to post it online, when the computer was booting up by itself. I could tell you about the time I confusedly went to talk to my brother at midnight about nothing in particular, but that I was desperate to talk to someone, and waffled emotionally until it was silly. I could tell you how beautiful my sister's head looked, and the size and wonder of her beautiful mind. I could tell you how I knew genius, and *was* a genius, and how for eight months I saw God everywhere. But what sense would that make to you? What could you take from that, and why would it be interesting?

You must know that it was a great time of my life,

that I was full of such hope and amazement, that a stronger person would have made the utmost best of the situation. Me, actually, I fucked it up really badly. Beyond belief, actually.

The night before God disappeared forever, he sung to me a lullaby in the form of the tune that Judy and I listened to the day we split up. It was Totally Confused by Beck. I knew when I heard it that God was saying goodbye. I cried that night and, for the first time in ages, in sadness. I wanted God to stay and asked for another chance.

It was bedtime. BBC News 24 was blaring out some conference in congress in America. In fact, Bush was giving a speech and I resolved to take notes with a view to writing some essay, comical or serious or ironic, whatever, to post to the website the next day. My head was lit with a burning desire to do that, and I had a thousand ideas a second and I was going to write the funniest political satire and send it to America. The speech ended and I fell asleep.

The next day, February 19 2003, I got up and went downstairs to write. The world outside was white with snow, and it was snowing. The phone rang. It was Gary. "Do you want to do some cocaine?" he asked. I paused. Did I want to do any cocaine?

"I don't know," I replied with genuine intrigue. I had tried weed and hash and skunk over the last few months, and it was fine at the best of times. But I hadn't done coke in ages. "Come and get me," I said.

I was in a state of indecision. What I should have said was, "Gary, I've got some work to do." Yet I was wracked with curiosity. In fact, coke had been suggested, at times, in the words I thought were being said by God. I had imagined how the world would have been if I had taken magic mushrooms. In fact, I had really wanted to experiment with those. But cocaine? How would that look? I couldn't imagine. Maybe it would be okay? No, I shouldn't. I'll think about it.

Gary arrived in his car. We drove in the snowy roads back to a house of a friend of his, and all the while I was in a state of indecision. Do I? Don't I? I want to. I probably shouldn't. But now I'm fascinated. I tickled my chin. I looked for a sign from God. He wasn't talking. We got to the house. It was empty. Outside I had noticed the cat bowl. I had also noticed a small tree with red berries, and looked at the beauty.

We sat down, and Gary went to get the cocaine. The TV was on, and there was some old black and white detective film playing. I was looking for a sign. I looked in the videos in slots on the shelf; I looked at the phone and the numbers and letters on that. Gary racked up the lines.

"And the final shot was fired..." said the detective in the film. What does that mean? Final shot?

'If you don't do that line,' I said to myself, 'you can smoke as much weed as you like.'

"There you go, Dan," said Gary after snorting up his line. There were only two lines.

"I don't know!" I said.

"Fuck it then," said Gary. "I'll have it."

It didn't occur to me that there might be other times to take cocaine. It was now or never.

"No, no!" I said. "I'll take it. Why not? Fuck it!" And I snorted the line.

Totally Confused

After the policeman's feet situation, I was carted off to a psychiatric hospital in Harrow, and brought on to a ward by the rear entrance. I was stunned by the injection of antipsychotics still, yet retained an essence of that higher consciousness, brought on by relapse - independent thought. It kept me amused for a while.

The long corridor led down past several closed doors and to a reception area where another long corridor went off to the right. The policemen spoke with the nurse on duty, handed me over, and were gone. It was late at night. The ward was dark and empty except for one man who shared his cigarettes with me.

His name was Paul and he introduced himself as an arsonist. I spoke with him in the smoking room, we exchanged the usual pleasantries common to the type you have with fellow schizophrenics on first meeting, exchanged the usual information of drugs, how long we're in for, what we'd done to come in, exchanged advice on the best course of action in such circumstances, exchanged the knowledge that there was nothing wrong with us and that it was their drugs that made us ill, etcetera, etcetera...

Soon, my father had arrived. He had brought essentials from my flat, clothes, books, Nintendo gameboy advance, and tobacco. We were in the seclusion room (the rubber room), which was on the corner of the ward, and where you sleep the first few nights until they find you a bed. Dad was complimentary to me as he found out my version of things, agreeing that I probably shouldn't have been hospitalised. I mean we both agreed, but seemed to have forgotten the minor incident at his football club a few days earlier.

I had gone along to sit with his friends and have a beer, and dad's brother-in-law, my uncle Dave, visiting from New Zealand, was with us. The club is the Old Finchleans. A few of dad's friends were drinking and watching a game and chatting. I'm not sure exactly what they chatted about, but probably football – something I had no knowledge of, and couldn't join in. Left to my own philosophical thoughts and watching the dynamics of the game, I sat as patiently as possible, which for a good five to ten minutes was very patient, considering the sort of thing going on inside my brain.

Earlier that day I had gone on a massive wander. I had awoken to the fact that, whether they knew it or not, the general public were reading my thoughts, and I was reading theirs. I had realised this whilst on some bus as I observed some passenger having some machination of mine: "This man is in love with me!" perhaps, or,

"Who said that?" or perhaps, "I'm a gay genius!"

My thoughts being audible, and at once fundamental, I realised that to have thoughts for the entire Earth was, in fact, my role.

It being the case that I had just twenty five pence in my pocket, and now being at the Totteridge and Whetstone tube station, and wanting to be in Mill Hill, I decided to walk along Totteridge Lane, which is a very long lane. Before I did, however, I remember accosting an older man, like an old builder in his fifties, and talking to him about whatever came into my head, perhaps how convenience shops sold Coca Cola, or how the cost of a bus journey is fifty pence, or how Descartes was a French philosopher. It was all obvious stuff, basic facts about life, and I thought he would tell me to fuck off, but actually he seemed deeply interested in everything I said, and even urged me to continue. In the end, I made my excuses and left.

Being psychotic - I mean, the actual state of psychosis - can be an enlightening experience. Some say good things about schizophrenia: that it is a sane reaction to a mad world, that you can have insights into the world that nobody else has. Others say that that is bullshit: schizophrenia is one of the most horrific ways biology can go wrong in a human brain. Today, however, psychosis wasn't so bad. As I walked down the lane I became aware of my central involvement in a tacit conversation between me, pedestrians and drivers of cars in the flowing traffic, and certain celebrities.

I mean, the bulk of thoughts I was having (and sharing) would probably be tedious to relate in their entirety, but to me each one was as enlightening as a night sky filled with stars on LSD. And, while each thought was different to the last, it seemed, in retrospect, like there was some theme; some psychotic insight that drove my mind; a feeling or impulse that I could use to succeed in world domination, or whatever success I was striving for, and I returned to it continually. I was turning thoughts around in my head, finding my way out of being by a new path, and using tacit communication with every member of society as surplus for talking to God. I would talk to God, and society would answer for Him, making the conversation real.

I walked Totteridge Lane, and I began to feel tired, and I decided to sit on a bank of grass. I don't know if doing such a thing was wrong, or if my conversation was that tedious, but just then, on a relatively mild day, there was a great crack of thunder and it began to pour with rain. I stood promptly, apologising profusely, and continued to walk, and came to a pond where I noticed some ducks – two of them – and I could read their minds. They eyed me humorously, as I recognised with surprise that they were thinking! "Oh my God," I said in astonishment. "I didn't know ducks could think!"

"What d'ya think we're doing?" replied one, with what appeared to be a knowing wink. The two floated on the surface of the water some way away.

"C'mere lads," I said and beckoned them with my

finger. They swam eagerly to the edge of the pond where I stood, in response. "You know," I began. "We eat you!"

"Get off!" said one duck in disbelief. "You? Eat us? I don't believe it!"

Of course! Ducks wouldn't believe that!

In any case, I would like to have stayed and shot the breeze with these fellows, but I was on my way, so I apologised for not having any food, said goodbye, and left. As I did, I turned around and saw a cow in a field over the road, watching me. I wondered if, like the ducks, cows could think. "You think, don't you?" I said to the cow.

"You're there," she said.

That's what cows say: "You're there."

I walked on, and I was in a field, and traffic was flowing by some metres away. In one passing van, I saw a friend from my building days, Ben. "There's Ben," I said.

"Do you see me talking to him?" he replied, to someone that wasn't me.

I was beginning to feel like the world had had enough of me, a thought that was confirmed by Steven Spielberg whose thoughts I was reading and with whom I would occasionally check in. The entire world knew that I was the central thinker, and it was an annoyance that the role had gone to me, a twat. Ben drove by.

The world was soured: It was slowly dawning on me that I was its messiah, and I was a failure, and the bane of this world, and everyone in it was working for me. In short, they wanted me dead.

At a turning near home, just at the top of the lane where my parents lived, I smashed my mobile phone and CD player in false frustration, and an attempt to get onside with the world. "I would've had that," said some man who witnessed me. I heard him think it.

I was home now, and mum knew I was unwell. She sat sewing at the table, not looking at me. I read her thoughts. "What's 'dice'?" she had said. 'Dice' was something I'd noticed about people's eyes that day. 'Dice' was where someone's eyes reminded you of dice. Mum's eyes were 'dice'.

"Dice is good," I told her.

So we were sitting at the club, me, dad, Dave, and all my dad's friends. And I'm watching the football up on the screen, and as I'm sitting there I notice the wooden frames on the walls, and the pictures of old teams, and so on, and I start to feel like I've been here before. All of a sudden I get this massive fucking déjà vu, and it comes over me like a shock. I realise that I've been here before, but the last time I was here I failed – failed something - and I realise that I've actually been here many times before, and I can't contain myself: I say, "Holy shit!" and I jump up from my seat, and I try to discourse about football, but I'm really excited, and I don't know anything about football! "Oh my God," I say. "Football is a game and there's two teams and you kick a ball about and you try to score and you try to win and the teams wear different colours and all the supporters love it and you try win and you to score goals and you kick a ball and...."

Dad had stood up and was ushering me out the door. "Come on, let's go home," he said. I looked around at the men. Dave was smiling. Others were smiling. 'What the fuck have I just done?' I thought. 'I've just totally embarrassed my dad in front of all his friends.' We left.

Now, two days later, we sat in the seclusion room of a psychiatric hospital, and what they had all said – "If you don't take your medication, you'll relapse" – had come true. I wondered if, by being here, I had let my father down. Being sectioned feels like the worst failure. But dad wasn't tuned in to that feeling. He was okay with it.

Harrow mental hospital was private, so it was good. You got nice meals throughout the day, and the rooms had en-suite bathrooms. The patients weren't too bad either. My first day there I met this dude that liked the same music as I did, and we listened to some of it in his room. He was this black dude with a Mohican and leather jacket. We listened to Pantera. There was this other Jamaican dude who looked like the meanest fucker in the world: he had red eyes and sat glaring at you while he smoked a cigarette, but he was alright. There was this one young chavvy sort of fellow, Paul or something, who said to me, "Can you read my mind?"

"Yes," I'd told him.

There was this Irish chap called Sean who was pretty

cool, and he was great friends with this other dude, a black kid called Immy, to whom I lent my gameboy, and he was pretty cool too. There was this other white bloke, James, who wore skateboarder's clothes, and kept himself to himself. Also, there was this French Muslim bloke who I didn't get on with at first, but soon came to befriend later on. And then there was Eugene.

Eugene was a monk. That's what he reminded me of. He had a massive rotund body and a bald head and he was a Cambridge graduate and he was a great man, and was always reading. I went into his room once, and it stank like a dressing room for a football team, but the smell was just Old Holborn. One day Eugene passed me a lighter. He had leave in the day, so he was able to smuggle one in. One day I realised being gay was the only way to get well, so I came out on the ward, and when I told Eugene, he kissed me.

One day my dad came to visit again because I had a meeting with the doctor, and Gary was with him. I was a bit annoyed with my dad. I mean, I had been all week. That's because I'd realised that he never answered my questions satisfactorily. I'd realised that all I needed was for him to say, "Because trees are green," whenever I asked him, "Why is the sky blue?" Coming up with answers was easy enough for me, but I needed to hear my old man give me some kind of answer. That day he was there, I confronted him. "Why is the sky blue, dad?" I asked.

"I don't know," he answered.

I began shouting at him in frustration, telling him he never thinks for himself and why can't you just say, "Because trees are green"? Anything! Any fucking bullshit, Dad!. Then Gary left and went and sat in the van, and the doctor called us in.

I had written a letter. Most of the time in hospital there I would write letters, and I had written one to the doctor. There was a whole panel of professionals in that room that day: doctors, nurses, social workers, priests. God knows what. And dad stood beside me as I requested that I read my letter.

It went on a bit, I'll admit. But the content was well meaning. In a few days my dad was to go to New Zealand to meet family and especially to see his old man, my grandfather Peter, who was dying of cancer; he would die any day. And I wanted to go. "I don't think that I'm that unwell," went my letter, "and I promise that I'll take my medication, and I'll behave, and my grandfather is dying and I'll never see him again. I know you think I'm unwell, but I'm not too bad, and I'll take my medication..."

The letter went on. It was repeating itself quite a bit. Before I finished there was a looming threat of an altercation when I wouldn't shut up and kept reading the letter: I felt I hadn't made my point. The nurses gathered around me as though about to drag me off to the seclusion room, and I wanted to finish reading my letter, to make my point, but dad calmed me down with a hand on my shoulder. "Hey, hey," he said gently.

"Daniel."

I calmed down to hear what the doctor had to say.

"You're psychotic."

No one had ever called me that before, and I could sort of see it. And as far as psychological assessments go, the doctor hadn't done a bad job of making me aware of my condition, although I was used to more convoluted approaches. But nevertheless, I was still slightly offended. I wanted to call the doctor homosexual to see if the same approach would work for him. However, I bit my tongue.

The doctor explained that I was too unwell to leave the hospital and that going to another country would not be possible. The news was not what I wanted to hear, but I could do nothing about it, and left the room. Dad stayed to talk to the doctor.

I walked down the hall and into the day room, thinking about my grandfather, and how I'll never see him again. And there I heard music that I'll never hear again, and didn't know what it was or who it was by, but it was this house and garage tune playing on the radio that was tuned to some pirate station. It sounded like angels, and it went:

I wanna be with you baby! I wanna be with you all day!

I wanted to cry, and I went to hide behind a wall because I wanted to cry alone, but the skateboarder dude was standing there, and the music was so beautiful, and I knew I would never hear it again, and I knew I would never see my granddad again, and I cried.

I wanna be with you baby! I wanna be with you all day!

"Why are you crying?" said James.

Then a nurse called Laura came in. She'd seen me upset walking in. "Why are you crying?" she said.

I didn't want to explain.

Before lobotomy - after coke...

I was back at home and reeling with confusion about why I had just been evicted from my Watford bedsit. Smoking cigarettes in my bedroom I watched Snatch, a gangster movie. It had inspired me to draw a picture of diamonds, but it was useless and I was frustrated. I was frustrated about the drawing, but mainly frustrated about the past, the present, and the future.

A few nights later, Gary and I went to a local bar for a drink. Some other Mill Hill types were in there too, blokes I had never been that friendly with. I drank in their surprise as I chatted with ease to the most attractive of women, making her laugh, and almost broaching the subject of taking her home. My strategy was to be as confident as possible, but the simplicity of approach was wasted in the wake of my three minute concentration span, and I became bored and went from woman to woman. I think I thought it was all too easy.

"Gary," I said as he gazed with distracted concern about the bar. "I bet I can go up to any table and make them laugh."

Gary shrugged. I went to some random table where there was a group of women and one or two young men. I proceeded to give some performance, for their entertainment, consisting of whatever random observations I had made, and they laughed, and I walked off, point proved.

Gary and I had a barney that night. Perhaps I was too lairy, or out of control, or perhaps I had made some unnecessary request of him, but when we left the bar, we ended up shouting at each other in the street. We nearly came to blows then, but it was a case where each of us was waiting for the other to make a move, but none of us did. Gary walked home. So did I.

The following day was a blur. I possibly slept in the entire time, but when the evening came I had the compulsion to go for a walk.

It was dark when I walked past the park. Sounds of the voices of teenagers drinking came from the playground. My back was tense, my head was fuzzy from frustration, and the teenagers had decided to start breaking chairs (as I could hear from the edge of the road). A recent resolve of mine was to not think, that is, to just feel, to just go along with the ebb and flow of the grain of circumstance, except is was less of an ebb and flow and more like a mechanical program. I wasn't out of control, though I was a robot, like the Terminator.

Another chair broke and I was compelled to deal with the perpetrator.

I turned left after the car park and walked slowly but purposefully up to the playground. There was a group of youngsters sitting on a fence. In this group there were mainly girls, but one lad in particular who I had unconsciously decided to attack. As I approached menacingly, the lad's eyes met mine, and he glared with bravado. Then, when I was about a metre from him, he cracked my intentions and bolted. I mean, he fucking ran. He ran far, and I went over the fence and went up to approach the next lad standing there. I wasn't thinking. I mean, I was just doing. I went up to that lad, and he bolted. Then I went up to the next lad (they were dotted about the area) and, well, he was one of those short cocky blokes, and he tried to show me impudence, as though he would have fought me, but he bolted too. By now, all the blokes were leaving the park; I had got behind them like I was rounding up sheep, and I was walking them out. There was about ten or so of them, in fact, and I still wasn't thinking. I was doing. If one of them strayed to the left, I would walk up to them on that side. "Psycho!" one shouted.

They wanted to have me, I knew it, and they could have if they could've organised themselves. Even a part of me was a bit scared. But when I thought to leave them to it, and made to walk the other direction, they would begin to walk after me. It was like a computer game. "Psycho!" the bloke shouted.

I had walked them out of the park, these ten or so lads, but one or two were still in the playground. As I crossed the car park, I felt an almighty whack on my right elbow. Someone from behind had thrown a lump of brick at me. I turned around but there was nothing I could do. The lads would have come back if I gave chase to the perpetrator. So I continued, walking them all through the streets and into town, actually really wanting to get out of the situation, and when I came so far, I was able to duck down an alleyway, by which time they were gone.

At the end of the alleyway, dad's friend Mo was having a party, which I knew about, and both my parents were at it. I went in saying how there was a load of kids wanting to beat me up. Mo got into his van and drove down to have a look. When he came back he was shaking his head, saying, "They were just kids, man!" That put it into perspective for me. It was true; they were just kids.

It was the next evening, and I was at home writing an email of sorts to Sarah, who was on her travels around the world. Whether I had been at home all day or possibly been labouring for my father on some job, I don't recall. But the email I was writing was not turning out to be very satisfying. Feeling a hunger of some kind or other, I decided to phone for pizza.

I got through and asked if I could have a medium margherita. Now here, with this simple request, there was some kind of misunderstanding, so enveloped in the abyss of masculine insecurity that the phone staff on the other end of the line decided to bar me. "You're barred!" he said and hung up. Perhaps I asked wrong? Perhaps it was me? Perhaps the man was stunned by the simplicity of my request that he was shocked into idiocy? Nevertheless, such a course of action made me very angry indeed. The following minute was one such that I realised my only option was to walk down to the outlet and have an argument with the offending person.

My body buzzed with the kind of aggression one always feels before a confrontation, as I marched in the direction of the town and the pizza shop. I muttered and cursed under my breath, with no doubt in my mind what I would do. I was going to lamp the fucker. Before too long I was in the shop. "What's your fucking problem?" I asked, directing the question at the brown headed young man as he ended a call. He looked confused. "I was just on the phone to you and you barred me. What did you do that for, you cunt?" I said.

"You were rude to me!" he explained when he remembered the instance.

"I was not fucking rude to you, but I'm gonna be rude now," and I spat at him. Then I swung my fist at his face, an action which did not connect, then spat at him again. This got the attention of some of the shop's workers, one of whom made his way around the counter, where I was, and was followed by our friend, the phone staff.

Now, I did not care a jot about the man that had

come to help, who was a stocky Greek man like the kind that work in kebabs, but he had walked in the front door to face me. However, I did care about the offending staff, the phone staff, who followed him in behind. The Greek standing in front of me, and the prick just beyond, I reached round with the best right hook I've ever swung, and it connected and got him right in the jaw.

That was it for me; I was satisfied. But a great rumble ensued with punches and kicks coming from all sides. Now another staff member had joined in. I found myself on the floor in the shop and, just as I started getting tired, I got a little sign from a word that I saw on a menu on the wall: the sign said INVINCIBLE, and I got a great boost from that. The fight continued for another thirty seconds but, there now being three of them, I was losing. In the end I wound up on the ground, with my jumper up over my head. They were now satisfied. They could have beaten me more, but they were satisfied, and that was that.

I got myself together and tried to catch my breath. There was no point in wasting any more time with those fuckers. I walked off feeling a bit battered. Something strange in me felt the need to end the night with a pint of lager, so I walked down Mill Hill Broadway, past the last night's bar, and on to the pub near the station. That walk is now an empty page in the journal of my mind, but I know I was struggling with questions of failure, pain, and frustration – and the questions were to God.

When I got inside the pub, I went to order a pint,

and did so with my last change. It was busy in there, and at the back I saw my brother's friends in a group, laughing and drinking. And soon, my brother himself emerged from the toilets, probably having just been admiring himself in the mirror, since he was throwing some gangster shapes to suggest that he had, and his friends laughed and drank. I took my beer, and with that same sense of aggression buzzing in my body, I tried to relax. I tried to avoid eye contact with any men in there because it only made me angrier. But I was immensely calmed when a young lady came and stood before me. I remember how I watched her body and wondered, and was sure of it, that she had noticed my stressed out state, and come to chill me out.

I struggled still with these questions I addressed to God, and the girl had gone, and I put my half-drunk pint on the table, and there being a train station across the road, I decided to leave and look for a high speed train.

"Is this what you want, Lord?" I asked as I approached the station entrance. A train pulled away, and I went through the gates. "You'd better stop me now, Lord, 'cause I'm gonna do it!" I threatened as I went up the station steps. The station was typically empty, and it being an overground station, I made my way onto the tracks. No train was yet in sight, but here they would usually come careening past at two hundred miles an hour every ten minutes, and I imagined one coming down the line and smashing me to pieces. "What now,

Lord? What now? If ever I needed you, it's now, Lord! Are you gonna talk to me now, Lord? 'Cause I'm gonna do it!" I said as I walked along the tracks.

"HEY!" someone called. I looked to my left. "HEY, GET OFF THE TRACKS!"

'Not bad, Lord!' I thought, as I saw a workman walking towards me. He was with two or three other workmen. My reaction was to kind of keep walking.

"Mate!" called the worker. "Get off the tracks! You can't!" Then he spoke into his walkie-talkie: "We've got a walker on the tracks, stop all trains!" or words to that effect. "Mate! Come back!"

The worker was part of a team, and they really helped me that night. In fact, when I did come back, they called on the services of some police (or whoever; I didn't know then), but these people never did arrive. And even when I walked off and went up the road, determined to kill myself somehow, and wound up on the tracks again, from a different route, and they had walked along the line and found me hiding in the bushes waiting for a train, they were *still* kind, and *still* helped me. No services came that night, no one who might have taken me in. I told the workers I was alright and I went home of my own accord, and went to bed.

I think I had slept in the next day too. Maybe I had had a day's work with my father. Whatever it was, that night I decided I needed either a fuck or a fight. I had thought I might get out of Mill Hill and go to a pub a bus ride away but, having no money, I decided to go back to the bar in the Broadway.

It was the beginning or my tirade against misogyny as I stood in the packed bar of Mill Hill, and looked for females to save. My resolution was that if I could beat up a man who appeared to be bullying a woman, then maybe she would sleep with me. A situation was not far away, and a man was indeed being mean to a lady. "Do you talk to all women like that?" I asked with a dead-eyed glare. The man had a hooknose and blonde hair, and visibly trembled when he explained that she was his sister. 'Yeah,' I thought. 'The woman'll really want to sleep with me after I've beaten up her brother!'

Having lost interest in him for that reason, I looked to my left and at the eyes of a young man who surely must have been just staring at me. It wasn't long before I had head-butted the poor bloke, at which a friend of his jumped at me. We rolled around the floor for a minute, and then the bouncers got involved. I stopped when I saw a drop of blood on the bouncer's lapel (probably put there deliberately and nobody's real blood). They took me aside.

Evidently, by my actions, I had pissed off a lot of people in the bar that night. I stood to one side as a group of men gathered outside. Two young lads chatted to me about appropriate fighting footwear for a minute, then, as a bouncer was explaining to me that I could go out the front way (where ten men wanted to kick the shit out me) or the back way, a big white dude with glasses came up behind him and punched me right in the nose.

"Motherfucker!" I said grasping my face.

"You can go out the front or the back," the bouncer said.

I was at the entrance, inside, when I mulled it over. 'If I go out the front,' I thought, 'then those men are gonna kill me'. And I thought, 'Well, that's something I probably need right now. And if I go out the back, then this phase, this issue I'm having, it will continue. I should go out the front, but – fuck it! – I'll go out the back.'

I did go out the back and that was really the sensible option, in all honesty. But I knew the group would find me, or thought they would, and I went up a stairwell and hid on a roof.

Eventually, I got home, but I was really disappointed. I still needed a fight or a fuck. I went to sleep with a feeling of unsatisfied frustration.

The next day my mum had asked me to go the job centre. That was the day I met old sledgehammer feet.

Thames Ward 2004 - The Golden Age

Medication makes you ugly. You see, that's really it. That's the whole issue about medication. We talk endlessly, as patients, about how antipsychotics take away your thoughts, make your mind dull, turn you into a zombie; about how one minute you were happily going about your business, and the next you were comatose in the corner, drooling and sparked, and not really sure what they've done to you. Patients talk for hours about not just the side effects of medicine – weight gain, lack of motivation, etc – but the actual effect of medication, which is a subject of fascination to us insofar as our main goal is to describe exactly what it's like to those who'll never have to take it. We talk about those things, and most times, we find ourselves acquiescing to the arguments of doctors, nurses, family and friends alike, who say that the treatment works for us. But in a nutshell, what we are actually trying to explain is that, despite the appearance of wellness, on the inside medication has made our brains ugly. I mean, as patients we remember having free thoughts, amazing capacity of insight, and so on, and despite whether we were well or not, as soon as drugs are administered, we can immediately tell that we've lost something special and we're never going to get it back. They say (you hear) that you can never take away what's inside. But mental health patients know deeply that that is fucking nonsense. They *can* take and very much *do* take away what's inside.

On the other hand, when you're in a hospital on some ward or other, you do meet some really funny characters, and perhaps their medicated state goes some way to add to the funniness.

After coming out of Harrow I was transferred back to Dennis Scott Unit in Edgware and put on Thames Ward. I remember walking in with my guitar and bag and immediately being approached by a young man called Keith, who I had met here the first time of being admitted, and who wanted me to play Oasis songs. "Ah, cool man! We can jam!" he said with excitement. I immediately began strumming the chords to Wonderwall. A skeletal type of man, whose t-shirt was pulled up around his back and shoulders, skulked around the corridors barefooted. His name was Graeme. A short, pink faced, bald man stood smiling in glasses, by one of the doors. His name was Patrick. After I was shown my room I came into the smoking room. Here, a large, bald, Iranian man was sitting, not smoking, and looked like

Plato. His name was Meyer. From the smoking room I could see into the TV lounge, where a small Indian woman was sitting next to a large Muslim woman. "I used to be a genius!" said Meyer.

"Yeah, I can believe that," I replied.

Keith appeared in the room and asked for a cigarette. I gave him a cigarette. "Why you so bald?" said Keith to Meyer, with a comical tone.

"I'll fucking kill you!" said Meyer to Keith, with a touch less comedy.

"I'll do kung fu on you!" Keith threatened, with a manoeuvre and appropriate vocal cry. "Maybe I'll beat some hair on your head!"

Meyer got angry, jumped up from his seat, and booted Keith in the arse. "You bastard!" he shouted. "I'll kill you!"

I was trying my best not to laugh, and then a nurse came in and asked what was going on.

"They are teasing me," cried Meyer. The nurse escorted him out of the room, and Keith nursed his arse.

Dinner time was announced, and having finished my fag, I went into the hall. Graeme was stalking around and was trying to hug me. He would walk towards me as though he was a zombie, and I'd scuttle off a few steps and look over my shoulder as though I was scared, and this process would repeat several times. Graeme wasn't retarded, but was waiting for his medication to kick in, which would take a week or so, so his speech was slurred, and he looked at you with his head tilted on one side.

"He liked that game you were playing," said Patrick, about Graeme. "Yes, that was a good game."

In the dining room all the patients sat quietly at tables eating their particular meals. "I am beginning to suspect that there is a higher power!" called Meyer in his Indian accent. He was sitting at the back of the room next to a Jewish guy whose name was Moshe. Moshe muttered some words of agreement.

Later, in the TV lounge, the small Indian lady sat with the large Muslim woman. I walked in and said, "Do you ladies believe in God?"

"Oh, yes, yes," they replied.

"Then it is time for us to pray," I said. "Repeat after me: 'Oh, God!'"

"Oh, God!" repeated the ladies.

"Oh, God, God, God!" I continued.

"Oh, God, God, God!" said the ladies, with a smile.

"Oh! Goddy, God-God, God-God, Goddy, God-God-God!" There came some humoured mumbles from the ladies. "Oh, Goddy, God, God-God, Goddy, Goddy, God, God, Goddy-God! Please! Please, God! Please!" The ladies smiled. "Amen!" I cried.

There was a new girl on the ward a day or so later. She sat in the smoking room with two children and a black dude. Hannah, as she was called, had just tried to jump in front of a train. She was a short girl with strawberry blonde hair, and spoke with a rasp. Hannah would become friends with a woman called Debbie who at first I thought was a nurse, and was always on her phone, and was a bespectacled Jewish woman in her late thirties, and introduced herself as a consultant. One night Debbie bought Chinese for everybody, and even sent some in a cab to Hannah's mother. Debbie was convinced I had an oedipal complex. One night we sat watching TV and she stroked my arm the entire time, like she was my mother. I think she thought she was my mother.

Debbie, Hannah, Keith and I were in the smoking room one night. There was talk of someone having an ecstasy pill. "Perhaps we should take it, and sit here fucked," I suggested.

"You know what I *mean*," said Keith animatedly.

We didn't have the ecstasy pill – I don't know what happened to that – but we sat there in the smoking room one night, and it was as if we *were* on ecstasy, chatting and joking. I remember Debbie smiling at me with relief every time I smiled at her. Debbie sort of fell in love with me, I think. I turned to Keith. "You," I said, "are a wise philosopher." Keith's eyebrows raised. "You," I went on, "are a great teacher." His eyes became soft with amusement. "You," I continued, in response to his look, "are a wise and great teacher of philosophy." Keith couldn't help but grin with happiness, and I continued to flatter him for some ten or fifteen minutes, with every different combination of the words 'wise,' 'great,' 'teacher,' 'philosopher,' and any others I could think to add. I remember Keith's impressed and flattered expression.

One night in the TV lounge, a Saturday night, I

think, I watched some game show, and Meyer was in the room, and some others were. "You know," he began suddenly. "My balls are very embarrassing."

"Are they?" I said.

"Very big; very embarrassing..."

Silence.

"You know," said Meyer. "If my balls were fruit, they would be plums. Very big they are."

"Really?" I said.

"Very big, they are: my balls. Very big."

Silence.

"You know," said Meyer after a moment. "In two minutes time, the world will be made of pure pink."

"Oh, pure pink?" I asked. "What makes you say that?"

"Because everything will be made of pure pink... everything will be made of pink."

Silence.

"You know," said Meyer. "These men on television are very attractive... They are like flowers to me..."

"Are they?" I said.

"Very attractive... very attractive..."

"Do you think you could be having a sexuality crisis?" I said.

"They are very attractive... very attractive."

More silence.

"You know, this man on television right now," said Meyer. "He is like a... a *star man!!*"

Everyone in the room laughed.

The rest of my time in Thames Ward I spent drawing, reading, and writing, and gradually I was allowed outside for longer and longer stretches, and people began to go home, and new people came in, and Graeme's medication kicked in and he was like a normal person again, and people left, and new people came in.

The night before the ward round in which I was supposed to be discharged, Keith knocked on my door. He had a small amount of skunk weed and he gave it to me. I took it, reluctantly, and smoked it in my room, and was so fucked by it that the next day at the ward round the doctor could tell something was wrong, and I was kept in for an extra week.

However, a week later, I was straight again and everything was fine, and I got to go home.

Back to the Future

And it was a dark time indeed. Somehow, by some back route or other, avoiding the main street, I got home to Colindale. But despite the events of the day – attacking several people, including students and random strangers, and deciding to never go back to university – I was still fuming with anger; the type of psychotic anger that won't go away. That evening, as I stewed in my flat, I realised I hadn't had enough.

I was drawn, by some compulsion, to leave the apartment and catch a bus to go to Hendon. I got off at Hendon Central, fuming, and punched the first man I saw.

"What for, man?" he cried, this little Indian businessman. I looked at him as if to say, 'You know what for,' and walked on.

Getting to the underpass, two men chatted on a bench and, as I went past, I made an intimidating motion with my arms as if to say, 'You want some?' The bigger man, a bearded Iranian, made the same motion back. So I walked up to them. "Come on then, you cunt!" I said, motioning him to make the first move. His friend was a bit more wary of me than the first, and then the two were joined by a third man who had just witnessed me hit the Indian businessman and had followed me down. I realised it was three to one and jumped into this kind of martial arts stance, bouncing up and down, as if I knew martial arts. "COME ON!" I yelled, and the second guy was really wary.

A few weeks ago, before university, I was beaten senseless by seven nineteen year olds not five feet from this spot. That beating was my fault, as usual: It had been one of those days; I was pointlessly angry, and deliberately bumped into one of them as I got to the end of the subway. For no apparent reason, when the lad said, "Watch it, bruv," I tackled two of them, throwing them halfway down the underpass. And then five more boys came round the corner. Anyway, long story short, they had kicked the shit out of my head, and broke my nose. So I think I was scared this would happen again, and I backed down from this fight. "WANKER!" went the bigger bloke, which didn't help my ego. I went home.

Back at home I stewed in my room, thinking about how I had just pussied out of a perfectly good opportunity to let off some steam. And I realised I hadn't had enough. The night was dark, and I went out of the flat again, and walked up to the parade of shops in Colindale. The anger was peaking. I passed various people whom I could have attacked, which angered me more and, lest we forget, there were still many closeted homosexual misogynists around the place. Walking past a betting shop, I spied one inside, sitting with his friend. I burst in. "Wakey wakey, you fucking cunt! It's time for your fucking breakfast!" I said aggressively. I went over to him and swung a right at the confused bloke's head. But he recoiled backwards, so it didn't connect. He and his friend rushed away from me, and they were both big blokes, but they were visibly scared and edged out of the shop backwards as we argued about what was whose problem. As I walked out after them, I saw a kid who lived on my block. He looked at me as if to say, 'Oi! You're a hardnut!' The friends walked off saying something about a gun, and then I realised I was a bit fucked. They were going to come back for me and do me in. I couldn't go home; I'd be followed. So I started walking to Edgware.

It was when I was at the Burger King that I realised I was being pursued. This huge black dude was following me slowly, and I couldn't hide anywhere – black dudes kept coming from the shadows. The man finally caught me up. He was five feet away from me, and traffic was everywhere. "Somebody let you out of somewhere?" he said in this deep, frightening voice, with these deep red eyes. I panicked, knowing I wouldn't have a chance against him, and I started knocking on car doors for help. I even tried a few handles.

"Help me!"

I dodged through cars until I was on the other side of the road, then all of a sudden I realised I wasn't being pursued anymore; the big dude had stopped following me. But I also realised I wasn't well. I had a mobile phone with me and called for an ambulance. They told me they would be there soon.

And after ten or fifteen minutes there was an ambulance, and I was relieved. I thought I was saved, but the ambulance seemed to park up for thirty seconds, then leave. It was an occurrence that did not serve to assist my situation. I shook my head in disbelief as the paramedics drove away, and I resolved to go directly to the hospital. It was close by.

It was about eight o'clock when I rang the ward's buzzer. It was Wellhouse ward at Dennis Scott Unit, and I was let in. I spoke to someone at the desk, out of whom I did not get much information. I wanted to stay. "I'm not well," I said to some nurse. "I need help."

No one was listening. The ward was quiet. There was a bearded male nurse. "I'm unwell," I explained to him. "I'm dangerous. I'm not well. I need help." The nurse looked me up and down. 'Am I supposed to beat this guy up?' I asked myself.

"From what I've heard," said the male nurse from the hallway, "you can go." My confused glance did nothing to change his mind. "Go!" he said. "Go! Go home!"

So I left.

I sat on a bench outside and called Gary. He was too busy to pick me up, but he gave Reggie a call, and Reggie drove to get me and was there within ten minutes. On the way back I got Reggie to go into the shop, next to the bookies where I hit that dude, to get tobacco or something. He came out telling me that they were talking about me in the shop. "One guy was saying, 'the punch didn't connect, but if it did he would've knocked the guy out!'" said Reggie. He dropped me home and came inside, and we were talking about the computer, and the whole time I was thinking, 'Am I supposed to beat Reggie up?'

But I didn't beat Reggie up, and he went home, and I went to bed.

****

Gary was supposed to come over the next day. We were supposed to have a spliff in the evening. That was the plan. There is a blacked out part of this day that I do not know what happened. But, like in a dream, I come to, angry as ever, walking back from somewhere in West Hendon, along the road to my flat. It is rush hour traffic and I'm walking along, angry as ever, and there's this dude walking the other way. He's a black dude with glasses, and he's smiling at me; grinning friendlily. Probably for that reason, I decide to attack the guy. I've seen the guy before in the area, and I scowl at him, and I run to punch him, but he's quick and he darts off into the road. But he runs into the path of a van, and the van has to brake hard, and does so, and the car behind crashes into the van, and the dude runs away down the road. The guy in the passenger side of the van looks at me as if to say, "You're a hard nut!" In any case, I realise I'm in trouble and scarper over a wall and go home.

But I'm not well. I'm still not well. And I don't know what it is I'm supposed to be doing about it. Inside the flat, I'm stalking about the place, wondering why I'm picking on all these black dudes.

Then I realise.

It's that fucking Kevin Howard. This whole thing is about that time I could've had a go at him, but didn't. This is about me pussying out of a fight with that Kevin bloody Howard.

Fuming, I pick up my dumbbells and start lifting. 'If I want to sort this out,' I think, 'I'll have to find Kevin Howard.

There's a hammer on the bed.

It's a small sized hammer that I bought last week for sticking pins in the wall, but...

There's a hammer on the bed.

I put down the dumbbells. I put on my trench coat. I pick up the hammer. The hammer fits snugly into the left lapel, and I can hold it there with my left hand in my left pocket, upside down. I leave the house.

The plan is to walk around until I find Kevin Howard, but my belief is that society will help me. That is, in my head, people in traffic that see me walking around will answer me, asking them if they've seen this bloke, and yes I have – go this way. Have you seen this bloke? Yes I have – go this way.

I go up towards West Hendon (because, well, I don't *really* want to hurt anybody – I'm just psychotic. I'm just unwell), but the traffic tells me to go to Edgware.

Have you seen this bloke? Yes, I have – go this way. They're on my side, these guys.

I walk past a petrol garage. There's a dude getting in his car. Is that Kevin? No, but Kevin is fucked. I've got a hammer in my trench coat. I could cosh anyone. Anyone. I could cosh anyone I see. Imagine how many people I could kill tonight? They'd thank me for it in the long run. They'd go straight to heaven. Life isn't real anyway. Life is pain. I'm just speeding up the process. Have you seen this bloke? Yes, I have – go this way.

There's a black-out for a while. Did I get the bus or did I walk to Edgware? I think I walked, but maybe I got the bus. I think I did get the bus. Four people walked on that bus without paying. I have it in my head that Kevin is going to turn up at a kebab house on Whitchurch Lane.

I'm at the kebab house. I've got fifty pence, and I order a diet coke, and I sit down, and I drink the diet coke slowly, and I've got a hammer in my trench coat, and I wait.

Five minutes, ten minutes later, and Kevin hasn't shown up. Some other black dudes come in, and I think about hitting them, but I don't, and it dawns on me that Kevin isn't going to show, and I leave.

And I walk down to the station, and I'm not well, and I know it. I'm dangerous, and all I can think about is attacking someone, and dudes walk by, and I don't attack them (because I don't *really* want to hurt anybody. I'm just psychotic. I'm just unwell), but every time I don't attack someone the anger increases, and the compulsion to cosh gets bigger.

I walk past some policemen who are getting into their car, and I look at one as if to say, "You better find some reason to arrest me, because I've got a hammer in my trench coat, and I'm psychotic." The policeman looks concerned but has no reason to do anything, and I keep walking.

Dudes walk by and every time I don't attack them the compulsion gets worse, and furthermore, the dudes get cockier and cockier. And Kevin's nowhere to be seen, and I haven't seen the dude in years, fuck it I'm going home. And I sit at a bus stop; the one that takes me to my parent's house. There's this dude, and he's at the bus stop, and he's the cockiest black dude yet, and I think, 'You know what? It's not just Kevin. It's any black dude.' And I resolve to attack someone before the night is over.

I get to my parents house, and mum lets me in, and I've got a hammer in my trench coat. I go into the back room and dad is sitting there watching Chelsea, and his head is there as I approach him from behind, and I think, 'Am I supposed to attack my dad?' Mum is pottering around in the kitchen, and I know she knows I'm unwell, but she doesn't know how unwell I am, but *I* do because I've just seen the image of what could have just happened in my head, and I'm filled with dread, shame, and guilt. I sit with dad and watch Chelsea. If I heard voices, they would be saying, "Kill someone,"

"Do someone," "Do some cunt," but for me they are messages from the television, in particular, the voices of the commentators. They really want me to hurt someone.

Also, my mind reading skills are at their strongest. Mum is pottering around in the kitchen, and she says something to dad, and dad replies, but I can read my dad's mind, and what he's just said is, "Do her mate, she's a fucking idiot." But I know he didn't really say that, but my mind reading skills are strong, and I can see the image of what could have just happened, in my mind, and I'm filled with dread, shame, and guilt.

The psychotic anger is overflowing, and there's nowhere for it to go, and some commentator on television has just said, "Do some cunt." So I get up and walk out of the house, thinking I've got no choice but to "do" someone.

I'm a little way down the road when dad calls out to me, "Daniel! Do you want a lift?" I feel a little relief when he says that, and I go back, and I get in the car, and dad drops me home.

The Chicken Shop Incident

I've studied Plato. I studied some for college where I wrote an essay about the history of Greek philosophy. Plato's idea was the theory of forms: it's where every physical idea on Earth has an archetypal origin in a metaphysical world. I always interpreted that world to be heaven. I believed in heaven for some time, and I wanted to go there. In my head I could almost see the heaven I wanted to go to. It was so close. The heaven that once was.

There's this movie, Constantine. It's where Keanu Reeves is an exorcist – he fights demons and fights Satan. But the main idea about that movie is that, if you kill yourself, you go to hell. I'd seen Constantine before I tried committing suicide, so I *knew* that, but I guess I didn't care. In any case, I'd failed in that endeavour, and I was still here on this shithole planet, with its suffering and meanness, so what way out was there? I had an idea of heaven.

And if you had an idea of heaven in your head, and it seemed like a nicer place than this one, and you quite liked it, you might want to go to that place. Wouldn't you?

There was a way of doing it.

I sat down at my desk and logged online, and I went into a chat room, and back then it was Yahoo chat. The particular room was a religious one. These guys had helped me before. I had one time been invited into a secret room full of beautiful mind geniuses, and this was at a particular low point in my life, and they'd been there, these geniuses, and saved my life with the written prayers of the truth of the knowledge of the one true God. And I'd cried. In fact, I was always searching for that same room, and I hoped I could be helped again, such that now I needed saving more than ever. There were no geniuses in this room, however. Just hillbillies and Muslims. I searched for an hour or so and gave up. I switched off the laptop.

My head was tense, and I was filled with psychotic darkness – one might call it an evil dread. And I lay on my bed and closed my eyes, that my mind might leave me be for a night. And I drifted into the unconscious. Yet the hour in a chat room, and the fear and dark thoughts of the day, turned like rusty cogs in my mind, and just on the cusp of sleep, like that moment in the yard of the Dennis Scott Unit where I thought I'd died, an image became visible to my inner eye, of that secret chat room, and in a sudden shock I saw a chat room page of geniuses all writing their same demand: "Tears, please." Yes, they would want that objective. But what tears were they talking of? Their desire was tears of joy, yet I had nothing to be joyful about. But such a request could not be dismissed, and I knew the time had come, and I had to die. I was ready to die. I snapped out of the vision with a jolt, clapped my hands together and, realising now I had no choice, I gathered up my trench coat and hammer and left the flat.

The winter night was dark and cold, yet the fact of this resolve made my signs happy. Flapping headlines in newspaper trash would sing my praises: "Star!" "Our man's done it!" and all other such surreptitious allusions to the glory of violence. I viewed them with a sense of relief, yet a sense of suspicion and cynicism.

The glory of violence? I remembered a saying from Bertrand Russell: "Sex is love." And, mentally, the logic of such a maxim turned itself from that through "sex is violence", to "violence is love", and I saw the truth of it for myself, and felt it, and felt dread and clear shame at the horror of such a world as this. And I wanted to leave it.

And now, hammer in trench coat, I had a mental picture of the scene of expectation. The victims, or rather, the players in the scene – those whom I would employ to act out my desires – would be a group of men; Colindale types (although, Brixton would be probably more an appropriate area – but there's no time to travel now), tough, burly youths, defensive and neurotic, yet with the strength to finish the job.

Yes, that really must have been the subconscious plan all along. For as I wandered up the wet streets and onto the parade at Colindale, I passed very many types of men whom my heart would not have hurt. An old Indian man viewed me with suspicion and fear, as I glared into his eyes with a mixture of psychotic anger and helplessness. An old Irish man staggered from a pub and tripped into the street, and muttered something meaningless, as my heart sank into my knees at the cowardice of what I was going to do.

A group of burly men was the image of my ends, and then, as I drew upon the window of a shop front, I saw such a group of men. But they were not half as burly as the men in the image of my mind. Yet their numerousness, the fact of their group number being just that of the one in my head, and the clothes they wore, their shoes, their laughter – it was just the right type of group that could help me achieve my ends. "They'll do," I said to myself, with the type of voice reserved for thugs, and went into the chicken shop, and stood at the bar.

At that time, I wouldn't have realised the pain of recalling how young these men seemed, as I viewed them from my stance. There were six of them, in sporty street clothes, and I suppose that, in psychosis, there is much less question about particulars, and I was psychotic, and my head was tense.

“Alright mate?” chirped one guy, an Indian chap, and in just that happy kind of way, and I cannot turn it any other way. It wasn’t a threatening greeting, nor was it tinged with aggression. It was just a happy guy saying hello.

‘You’re fucked,’ I thought, as I nodded in response. The staff behind the counter was taking orders from another customer in the shop, and I wondered how I would go about my actions. Out of the six guys there, I had made my mind up to single one of them out, and he was the one I thought the hardest, and he was the black dude in the group, and now I can see him, smiling at some joke, with no idea about what was going to happen.

I stood at the counter and wondered how I would go about this course of action, as I watched this group of guys – this group of guys that my mind was convinced were ruffians or bad people or gangsters. But they were just kids. They were just kids, man. My mind was made up, though. But that makes it sound like I knew what I was doing. And in choosing what I was supposed to do I fell into my familiar method: the bane of my life; the two words I said before making every bad decision of my life – before leaving school; before taking marijuana; before taking ecstasy; before taking cocaine; before taking medication – the two words that would satisfy my unconscious need to do as I please. “Fuck it,” I said as I pulled out the hammer.

I can remember the poor dude’s face as the hammer swung over an arc of distance and landed clinically on the crown of his skull. It was not anger. It was not even pain, really. It was surprise. His expression was that of: 'I can't believe what just happened to me.' His mouth fell open, and he looked into my eyes of insanity, and even in my insanity, at that point I've never felt more guilty of any action I have ever done in my entire life. It made my next action all the easier.

The guys were ruffled, to say the least, and shocked, and the chap who had greeted me said, "What the fuck?!" And he started pushing me back, trying to get the hammer from my hands. It was a simple enough task for *him*, I'm sure, and I could sense the confusion of such simplicity, as I basically and equably handed him over the hammer. I could feel his confusion in that.

But now, it was their struggle to act in conflict with their intuitions; their confusion was immediately lost in the fission of their reaction, which was to batter me senseless.

I've never felt pain like it.

The first blow came striking down on my skull, and I went down, and blood spattered on the tiles at my knees. I thought it was the other guy's blood, but it must have been mine. Also, I felt my skull crack and noticed, as well as the open feeling of my mind (natural to being off medication), a sense of relief. We all desire resolution in our lives, and this felt like the end of an epoch.

The second blow came, and now, by instinct rather than by an effort to protect myself, my hand was covering my head, so they'd got my hand. I felt like Jesus in a hole, trying to crack a smile.

The third blow came.

The fourth blow came. It was as if they were all having a shot. Perhaps I *had* chosen the right group after all. Was there shouting? Perhaps the cheers of geniuses (their precious tears). They were not done yet. And light poured from the cracks in my skull, and I wondered if I would see heaven tonight.

I had been a rabid dog, crawling around the floor of the cage of the earth. I had been a jester, knelt at the feet of a clown. I had been a false bishop, bathing and sipping in Satan's piss. My dusty mind clamoured at the images of paradise, that rend your heart in loneliness, as my knees slid about in blood. That black freedom, which we mistake for the outside world, which we drive to conquer, which in my case is full with neon artificiality, well, I saw it for what it was. Now there was just a ghost, and it was my master, and here it came with open arms.

However many blows after that, I could not tell you. But as I genuflected before these buzzing men, these furious wasps of men, I heard the voice of my original victim gruffly and angrily say, "Gimme that hammer..."

I have made some very bad choices in my life. *I* have done many terrible things in my life.

THE END

Printed in Great Britain
by Amazon

44355131R00165